LOWE'S
Improving Home Improvement

creative
ideas
for
outdoor living

LOWE'S COMPANIES, INC.

Robert Niblock, PRESIDENT, CEO,
AND CHAIRMAN OF THE BOARD

Melissa S. Birdsong,
DIRECTOR, TREND AND DESIGN

Zach Miller, MERCHANDISER

Bob Gfeller, SENIOR VP, MARKETING

Jean Melton, VP, MERCHANDISING

Mike Menser,
SENIOR VP, GENERAL MERCHANDISE MANAGER

Dale Pond, SENIOR EXECUTIVE VP,
MERCHANDISING AND MARKETING

Peggy Rees,
CUSTOMER RELATIONSHIP MANAGER

Anne Serafin, MERCHANDISE DIRECTOR

LOWE'S CREATIVE IDEAS
FOR OUTDOOR LIVING

René Klein, PROJECT DIRECTOR FOR LOWE'S
CUSTOM BOOKS, SUNSET PUBLISHING
CORPORATION

Stephanie Patton, DIRECTOR,
SPC CUSTOM PUBLISHING

Catherine Hall, ACCOUNT MANAGER,
SPC CUSTOM PUBLISHING

Alice Lankford Elmore, EDITOR

Michael MacCaskey, WRITER

Sally W. Smith, CONSULTING EDITOR

Jennifer Allen, ART DIRECTOR

Amy R. Bickell, Melissa Hoover, DESIGNERS

Lynn Ocone, PHOTO EDITOR

Rebecca Bothwell, COPY CHIEF

Paula Hughes, Don Koenig, COPY EDITORS

Scott Kennedy, PRODUCTION MANAGER

Frank VonBechmann, Lois Chaplin,
PROOFREADERS

Nanette Cardon, INDEXER

Cover: Even a single chair on a tiny patio can be transformed into a beautiful outdoor haven for reading or relaxing. Photo by Friedrich Strauss/ The Garden Picture Library.

10 9 8 7 6 5

First printing February 2003
Copyright © 2003 Sunset Publishing
Corporation, Menlo Park, California 94025.
First edition. All rights reserved, including the
right of reproduction in whole or in part in any
form. Library of Congress Control Number:
2003102967. ISBN: 0-376-00919-5. Printed in
the United States.

Photo Credits:

Left (L), Center (C), Right (R), Top (T), Middle (M), Bottom (B)

Teena Albert: 28; Jean Allsopp: 7, 53TR, 65B; Ralph Anderson: 104TR; Scott Atkinson: 14B; Brian Baer: 26TL; Liz Ball: 60TL; Mark Bolton: 99TL; Marion Brenner: 13TL, 24, 27T, 73BR, 90C; Gay Bumgarner: 27BR, 60TR, 80BR, 84TR; Karen Bussolini: 70CR; James Carrier: 79CR, 95TL; Jennifer Chandler: 90T; Walter Chandoha: 60C; Van Chaplin: 8, 9, 10, 22BR, 29T, 34, 36, 37, 48, 49, 50, 52TR, 57CL, 57TR, 59CL, 62, 63BL, 65TR, 66, 67, 68TR, 68TL, 68CL, 70TL, 71, 74T, 75T, 75B; Claire Currans: 23BR; Robin Cushman: 6, 31; R. Todd Davis: 59TR; Andrew Drake: 57BL; Ken Druse: 12; Derek Fell: 57TL, 57CR; Scott Fitzgerrell: 102TL, 102ML, 102BC; Roger Foley: 20, 56TR, 102BR; Laurey W. Glenn: 42, 43, 46T, 53TL, 53C, 54T, 63T, 65TL, 68B, 82TL, 92BL, 93, 94BR, 94TC, 96, 101R, 102; John Granen: 82TR, 92TL; Art Gray: 91T; Steven Gunther: 26TR, 30T, 55TL, 100TR, 101CL, 104C; Mick Hales: 59TL; Jerry Harpur: 25M, 25B; Lynne Harrison: 80T, 98CR, 107TR; Philip Harvey: 13B, 18, 44BL, 79TR, 83BL, 89C, back cover; David Hewitt/Anne Garrison: 76; Saxon Holt: 46BL, 58T, 64C, 72TR, 73T, 98TC, 100TL, 101TL, 106BL; Dency Kane: 58C, 73BL, 97B; Andrew Lawson: 83TR, 83MR, 99TR; Just Loomis: 95C; Mark Luthringer: 20; Jim McCausland: 61BL; Jack McDowell: 72TL; Peter Malinowski: 86, 87T, 87CL; Charles Mann: 30B; Sylvia Martin: 59CR, 68CR, 70TR; Alan Mitchell: 75CL; Terrence Moore: 56TL; John O'Hagan: 38, 40, 45, 46, 52M, 53B, 54B, 64TL, 78TR, 80BL, 83BR, 84TL, 92TR, 92CR, 94T, 94BL, 96, 104TR, 105TL, 105TC, 108B; Jerry Pavia: 22BL, 70BR; Phifer Wire Products: 50M; Norman A. Plate: 19, 23BL, 64TR, 79B, 102TR, 104CR, 106TR, 107CL, 108T; Ian Reeves: 69; Allen Rokach: 32, 33; Nancy Rotenberg: 89TL; Susan A. Roth: 70BR; 100CL; 100BL; Royal Design Studio: 61R; Jim Sadlon: 88T; Richard Shiell: 22T; 87CR; Smart Deck® No-hassle Deck and Railing Systems by USPL: 44T; Thomas J. Story: 26BL; 29B; 95TR; Friedrich Strauss/The Garden Picture Library: 27BL; Ron Sutherland: 25T; Michael S. Thompson: 72MR; Dominique Vorillon: 91BL; Jessica Walker: 50T; Deidra Walpole: 55B; Janelle Weaver: 88C; 88CR; Peter O. Whiteley: 99B; Suzanne Woodard: 84B; 89TR.

We KNOW What You're Looking For

Welcome to the first offering in our *Lowe's Creative Ideas* book series. If you're familiar with our magazine, *Lowe's Creative Ideas,* then you'll recognize some of the doable projects, handy tips, and inspiring photos that fill this book. If you're not yet acquainted with the magazine, we're sure you'll find this sampling of its great ideas as exciting as our subscribers do.

While we believe this book will inspire you, we also expect it will assist you in the process of planning, creating, and enhancing your outdoor living space. From time-saving tips on shopping for supplies to fun and easy projects you can do in an afternoon, *Lowe's Creative Ideas for Outdoor Living* will help you transform your yard into a place that reflects your personality.

Browse these pages, and you'll discover that a beautiful outdoor space is not about manicured lawns or professionally designed decks. It's more about determining your style, your budget, and the physical characteristics of your yard, and then working with all these factors to create an environment that is right for you and your home.

We hope that this book will motivate you to step outside into your yard, take a look around you, and think of all the wonderful things you can do to make the space comfortable and inviting.

For more great projects for your home and garden, look for the other two installments in this series—*Lowe's Creative Ideas for Organizing Your Home* and *Lowe's Creative Ideas for Kids' Spaces,* both available at Lowe's.

Melissa

Melissa Birdsong
Director, Trend and Design
Lowe's Companies, Inc.

P.S. If you are not already a subscriber to Lowe's Creative Ideas, *we invite you to subscribe. Please visit us online at* **LowesCreativeIdeas.com** *to request your free subscription.*

Enjoy the time you spend outdoors.

CONTENTS

128 AT LOWE'S WE'RE HERE FOR YOU

CONSIDER
THE POSSIBILITIES

J UST OUTSIDE YOUR DOOR is a place where you can relax in the shade of a flowering tree or challenge the youngsters to a game of touch football. Or perhaps your ideal spot is an intricately designed garden where you can lose yourself in the pleasure of coaxing flowers to bloom.

The photos here and on the following pages are sure to inspire you with visions of the different outdoor worlds you can create. They'll help you make the yard of your dreams a living reality.

For many, a yard offers a family-centered space that is a haven from the outside world. But it also can be a place to entertain dinner guests, play games and sports, and welcome neighbors and friends.

To enjoy all these aspects of outdoor life, designate areas of your yard for different functions, and then separate them from each other physically or visually.

LEFT: Sheltered by grapevines, this peaceful patio sets the stage for an enjoyable meal.
ABOVE: An arbor bedecked with roses creates an inviting entrance to this homeowner's lush yard.

WHEN YOU TURN THIS PAGE, you will begin learning the process of planning, creating, and enjoying your outdoor living area. In this section, you will see how to assess your situation and deal with its challenges. The section called "Make It Happen" will give you the basic information you need to make your dreams a reality, whether you dream of an elaborate deck or a secluded spot for relaxing. In "Enjoy Outdoor Living," you'll see all the great ways you can enhance your space with grills, furniture, lighting, water features, and container plantings. On these two pages, and throughout the book, you'll see a variety of beautiful end results you're sure to find inspiring.

But first you must determine your vision. Begin by thinking about you and your family. It's much better to plan a space to fit your natural habits than to have to worry about changing those habits after it's built.

If you don't like housekeeping, the landscape shouldn't require neatness. If children will play there, don't plan a yard that can't take punishment. How about teenage parties? Grandchildren? A good yard is like a good house—it should accommodate the people who live in it and adapt to their changing interests and needs.

Do you enjoy building things, or does the prospect of mixing concrete intimidate you? Will the rest of the family be happy to pitch in with the building, digging, paving, and planting?

Two important factors to consider are the size of your budget and how much leisure time you can devote to constructing your landscape. For many homeowners working on their own, a reasonable schedule might be two to four years. Be sure to factor in adverse weather and other problems that might cause delays.

WHAT YOU HAVE

TIME AND MONEY

Be realistic about how much time the project will take and the skills required. Decide whether or not you will require the assistance of a professional, at either the planning or the installation phase, or both.

Once the design is complete, double-check with your suppliers in order to make sure the necessary materials are available and that you (or your contractor) are comfortable using them. If you do use a designer and contractor, arrange for them to meet to go over the plan and materials and agree on a schedule. That way everyone will have the same understanding of the project.

Whether you have flowers, food, or just plain fun in mind, a beautiful and functional outdoor space takes planning. Consider the needs of each family member, as well as the time each is willing to contribute to the project.

these trees also might shade out your newly planted flowerbed.

TAKE INVENTORY OF YOUR SITE

Every property presents unique opportunities. But along with them come unique challenges. You'll need to assess these realistically, and then find a way to balance them with the features you want. The following pages will help you identify the important natural features of your site.

You'll also need to evaluate any manmade structures and existing plantings, especially trees and shrubs. Sketching out these features to scale on paper will give you a base plan, which will form the foundation of your design.

GIVE YOURSELF SOME TIME

If you've just moved into a new home, don't reach for your pick and shovel right away. Try to live with your yard for a full year. You'll get to know the site throughout the seasons and will have the chance to experiment with various plants. Thorough knowledge of the site will produce a better plan.

Keep in mind that sometimes it's necessary to be ruthless. There's no need to include a scraggly tree or an ugly fountain just because it's already there.

A final point—if you decide to develop just one area of the yard at a time, think about how the changes will affect the rest of your space. For example, a row of tall hollies might supply immediate privacy, but

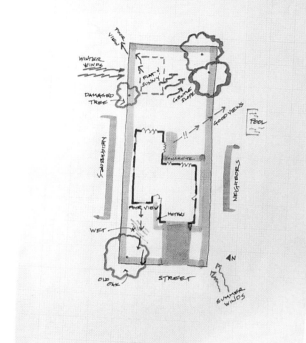

ABOVE, LEFT: If you are tackling some garden issues that are beyond your expertise, consult with a landscape architect or other garden professional. LEFT: This is a sketch of a base plan that a homeowner did of existing structures and landscaping elements in his yard.

You'll save yourself many hours with your tape measure by locating any of the following, which may be found with your closing papers or at the courthouse.

- a deed map that gives actual dimensions and the orientation of your property

- a topographical plan, with contour lines showing the exact shape and elevation of your site

- architectural plans giving the locations of all buildings

Lacking these, simply measure your property, and transfer the dimensions to your base plan, preferably on graph paper using an appropriate scale. After you finish, slip the base plan under a sheet of tracing paper, and sketch designs to your heart's content. This will allow you to try out ideas before committing yourself. (To learn more about this, turn to page 21.)

HERE IS AN EXAMPLE OF THE ADVANTAGES AND CHALLENGES OF THIS PARTICULAR SITE.

A. *The view from the living room is that of street traffic, passersby, and parked cars.*

B. *Damp pockets of soil can limit plant choices.*

C–D. *Warm summer air blows from the southwest (C); winter winds come in from the north (D).*

E. *Concrete terraces reflect summer heat into the home, but they are too small for entertaining.*

F. *Neighbors' homes are very close to the property lines, thus limiting privacy.*

G. *Gently sloping ground and existing trees can be incorporated into the planting design.*

H. *Open, sunny areas in the rear and on the south side yard offer space for a swimming pool or sun-loving plantings.*

I–J. *Rear views from the patio are pleasant in one direction (I), but unpleasant in another (J).*

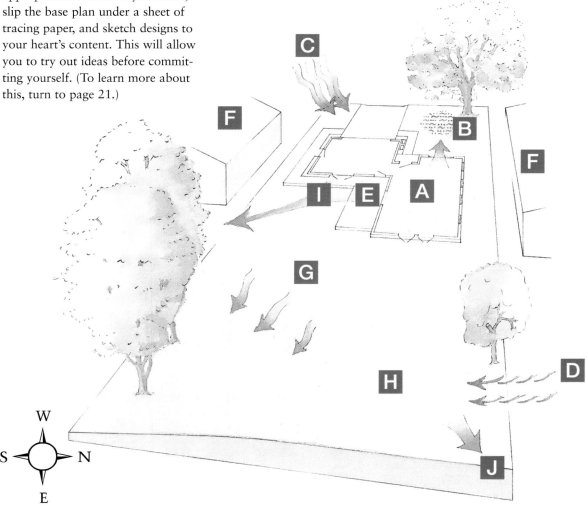

Your Piece of Land

What is the shape of your lot? How will its form affect your landscaping? Each lot shape has advantages and disadvantages.

A rectangular lot in the center of the block has its own limitations. The view of neighboring roofs and windows must be considered in your planning. The use of your backyard may be influenced by as many as five neighboring families. If, by some miracle, all five could get together on a program of tall shrub and tree plantings, privacy and sun and wind protection could be achieved more cheaply and efficiently than if each homeowner went his or her own way.

A long, narrow lot presents many advantages. You can easily zone it into areas according to use—outdoor room, children's play area, work center, etc. The design trick here is getting these areas to flow together harmoniously.

Pie-shaped lots, with the narrow end toward the street, are probably the most desirable. They give the least space on the street and the most space behind the house.

Corner lots present a trade-off. What you lose in privacy, you gain in a feeling of openness that you don't have with an interior lot. Compared to the interior lot, where you give up the setback space on the front only, the corner lot makes you give up both side and front to the public. Consider compensating with hedges or fences.

Indoor-Outdoor Relationship

The development of outdoor living space can give interior rooms an entirely new dimension. Check for garden views from each window of the house. Can a patio be built so that it is a visual extension of the

CLOCKWISE FROM FAR LEFT: These homeowners conquered steep lots with stone steps and terraced beds. A narrow lot is softened with a variety of plants and trees and divided into areas for relaxing. Walls of windows and ceilings crafted from arbors create rooms that merge the outdoors and indoors.

living room? Would a kitchen patio be more usable? If the indoor floor is above ground level, are the steps from house to yard easy to negotiate? A deck at floor level might make the living room appear larger and the entrance to the yard more attractive and useful.

Utility Connections

Before implementing your plan, answer these questions: Will sewer pipes or a septic tank drain field interfere with tree plantings? Is plumbing conveniently placed for future spigot needs? Should there be a faucet and/or a drain in the garden work center? Where will the hoses connect? If you plan to light the area at night, do you have outdoor electric service and weatherproof outlets conveniently located?

GETTING TO KNOW YOUR SOIL

Only the climate has a greater impact than your soil on the plants you can grow. Fortunately, soil isn't like the weather—if you don't like it, you can change it.

Soil is classified according to the particles that comprise it. Sandy soil has large particles, contains lots of air, and doesn't compact. Water and nutrients run right through it. Clay soil, on the other hand, has tiny particles. It holds water so tightly it forces out air, compacts easily, and dries as hard as a brick. Silty soil has intermediate-size particles and properties.

For most garden plants, the perfect soil is loam—a light, crumbly mixture of nearly equal amounts of sand, clay, and silt, with a good bit of organic matter added as well. Organic matter loosens heavy clay soil, allowing the penetration of air and water. It also improves the water- and nutrient-holding capacity of sandy soil. But soil texture isn't the whole story.

pH Requirements

One of the most important characteristics of soil is its pH—its acidity or alkalinity on a scale of 0 to 14. A pH of 7 is neutral; everything below that is acid, and everything above it is alkaline. Each plant prefers a certain pH, but most adapt to a range between 5.5 and 7.5. Soils with a pH below 5 or above 8 restrict the availability of soil nutrients. An accurate soil test conducted by your county Extension agent can help you get the most out of your soil, or you can use one of the soil test kits available at Lowe's.

If your soil has an undesirable pH, that doesn't mean you're stuck with it. You can add lime to overly acid soil or sulfur to overly alkaline soil, but you'll have to repeat the

Your soil will make the difference between a lush lawn with lovely blooms and a lackluster garden. A soil test lets you know what your soil needs to do its best.

additions periodically. If you don't want to go through this process, just choose plants that enjoy your existing soil.

Heavy Clay

Clay, also known as adobe or gumbo, is a gardener's curse. Ranging in color from red to brown to gray to black, soil that is mostly clay is heavy, drains poorly, and is hard to work. It's even harder for plants to survive in it. When clay soil is wet, it can't be worked, and plants rot. When it's dry, plants shrivel. But there are proven ways to improve clay soil over time. Every year, work in lots of organic matter—chopped leaves, shredded bark, composted manure, grass clippings, stable sweepings, or garden compost. Organic matter binds clay particles together into larger particles, allowing air, water, nutrients, and plant roots to penetrate. Also till in plenty of coarse builder's sand. If you can't amend the soil each year, build raised beds, and fill them with good garden soil.

Hardpan

Hardpan, known as caliche to gardeners in arid regions of the Southwestern United States, is an impermeable layer of earth that can be as much as several yards thick. It usually forms in areas that get only enough rain to dissolve minerals, most notably calcium carbonate, and carry them just below the surface, but not enough to wash them out altogether. These minerals then cement the soil together as it dries. A hardpan can also be formed by tilling clay soil while it's wet.

The closer a hardpan is to the surface, the more trouble it causes. It prevents the roots of plants from reaching nutrients and water, resulting in stunted growth or even death.

While no garden is maintenance free, good soil gives your plants a leg up and minimizes your sweat equity.

cold air pockets

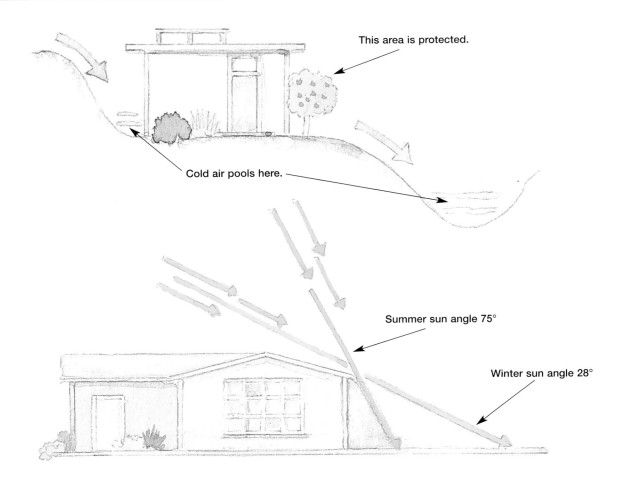

This area is protected.

Cold air pools here.

Summer sun angle 75°

Winter sun angle 28°

MASTERING YOUR CLIMATE

Almost every gardener knows the frustration of having a favorite plant freeze or fry, while the identical plant thrives in the garden across the street. This difference can be the result of microclimates.

Microclimates arise from a combination of factors, including the path and angle of the sun, the season, proximity of water, topography, and wind patterns. Most gardens produce several microclimates—areas that stay a little warmer or cooler, wetter or drier, more or less windy than others. Because these areas determine what you can grow, and how and when you can enjoy the garden, understanding how they work should be part of your planning.

Air Movement

Warm air rises, and cool air sinks. Thus, cool air tends to pool in low spots and behind obstacles such as hedges and walls, creating frost pockets. Slopes are the last places in a garden to freeze, because warm air flows up the face as it is displaced by the descending cool air. Flat areas, by contrast, cool quickly as heat radiates upward, especially during clear, still nights. Overhead structures, such as arbors and overhangs, reduce this heat loss and often protect the plants beneath them from frost.

Soil Moisture

Soil moisture has a profound effect on the local climate and growing conditions. Moist soil helps insulate tender plants in winter, because water emits heat as it freezes. Also, cold doesn't penetrate moist soil as deeply as it does dry soil. Moreover, moist soil cools its surroundings in summer as water evaporates. That's why summer heat records frequently occur during extended periods of drought. The lesson here is that sufficient soil moisture reduces temperature extremes.

Garden Structures and Paving

As gardeners with courtyards can tell you, what will grow inside the garden walls is vastly different from what will grow outside. In addition to blocking cold winds, walls store heat during the day (especially if they're made from a dark-colored material) and release

summer shadows

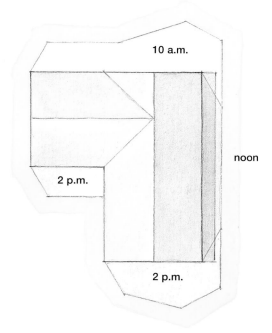

winter shadows

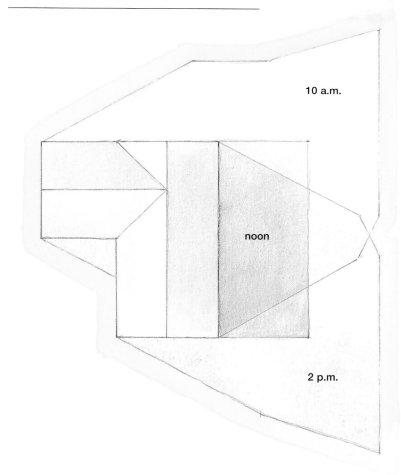

heat at night, keeping the enclosed garden warmer. Dark-colored paving stores heat too. As a result, plants growing near walls or paving tend to survive the winter better than those in exposed spots.

Sun and Shade

In summer, the morning sun rises in the northeast, arcs high across the southern sky, and sets to the northwest. This long passage means extra hours of daylight, which benefits many vegetables, annuals, perennials, and flowering trees and shrubs. By contrast, the winter sun rises in the southeast, passes low across the southern sky, and sets to the southwest. Days are much shorter, which triggers the blooming of short-day plants, such as Christmas cactus and bougainvillea.

That shifting sun angle means longer shadows in winter and shorter ones in summer (see illustration on opposite page). Thus, plants hidden in shade in winter often step into the sun in summer. The pattern of sun and shade also varies according to time of day. At noon, when the sun is highest, shade is scarce. So plan for these changes, lest one day you find a prized shade lover stewing in the midday sun.

Exposure

Slopes that face toward the south or southwest get more heat and light during the day than those that face the north or northeast. Similarly, walls that run east and west reflect extra heat and sunlight onto plants growing on their south side and less on plants growing on the north side. Heat lovers, such as crepe myrtle, forsythia, and lantana, flourish in full sun. But the soil obviously dries much faster in full sun, so be sure to provide a little extra water.

GETTING STARTED

NOW THAT YOU HAVE SOME IDEA of what you have and what you would like to have in your landscape, you might be wondering where to start and how much it will cost.

The truth is that there is no one way to landscape a yard. Some are planned by experts and installed over a few weeks or months, and others, without the support of professionals, may evolve over a few years. Nevertheless, all successful gardens begin with a plan. As to cost, you don't need to go high-end on every element of the garden. To achieve a feeling of luxury, you need only to take a step here and there beyond necessity.

Bubble diagrams are a useful method of planning spaces in your landscape. Using tracing paper over your master plan, draw activity bubbles. Overlap them where activities or uses will mix, and use lines to suggest walls, walks, and borders.

landscaping goals

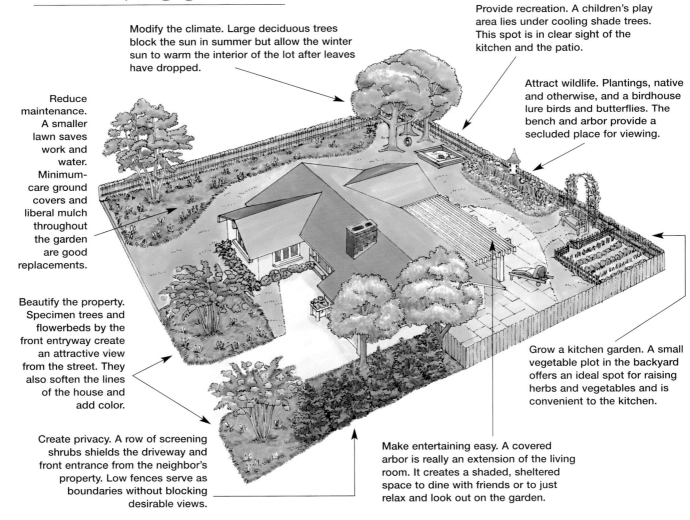

Modify the climate. Large deciduous trees block the sun in summer but allow the winter sun to warm the interior of the lot after leaves have dropped.

Provide recreation. A children's play area lies under cooling shade trees. This spot is in clear sight of the kitchen and the patio.

Attract wildlife. Plantings, native and otherwise, and a birdhouse lure birds and butterflies. The bench and arbor provide a secluded place for viewing.

Reduce maintenance. A smaller lawn saves work and water. Minimum-care ground covers and liberal mulch throughout the garden are good replacements.

Beautify the property. Specimen trees and flowerbeds by the front entryway create an attractive view from the street. They also soften the lines of the house and add color.

Grow a kitchen garden. A small vegetable plot in the backyard offers an ideal spot for raising herbs and vegetables and is convenient to the kitchen.

Create privacy. A row of screening shrubs shields the driveway and front entrance from the neighbor's property. Low fences serve as boundaries without blocking desirable views.

Make entertaining easy. A covered arbor is really an extension of the living room. It creates a shaded, sheltered space to dine with friends or to just relax and look out on the garden.

Careful planning will allow you to incorporate water features, pathways, beautiful plants, and a spot for relaxing into your landscape.

ABOVE: With some forethought and planning, you can create a permanent dining space that is functional, attractive, and durable. **RIGHT:** A triangular turf area adds interest to the landscape and also allows space for various seating groups.

PLANNING WITH A PURPOSE

Before designing or renovating an outdoor area, consider the kinds of activities you will most likely be enjoying there. Do you like to eat and entertain outdoors? Do you prefer to swim or to play basketball? Do your children need a spacious lawn on which to play? Perhaps you are more interested in relaxing in peace and quiet.

Be realistic about accommodating your favorite pastimes. A steep slope, for example, isn't suited to soccer. Raising ostriches in suburbia isn't practical or legal. And few neighbors will appreciate a concrete pad that's a permanent home to your collection of old cars.

Family Considerations

Your family's needs, now and in the future, will dictate many aspects of your design. For example, if your family includes small children or pets, plan for safety and ease of movement. Secure walls, fences, and railings can safeguard against dangers posed by swimming pools, driveways, busy streets, and elevated decks. Ramps and graded paths with smooth, firm surfaces ease passage for the physically challenged. Night lighting enhances safe movement and discourages intruders.

To make the yard more comfortable, you may have to modify the climate. Well-placed shade trees, tall screens, and verdant arbors offer respite from summer heat. Fences, walls, and hedges can buffer cold or salt-laden winds.

Gardening Goals

Most gardeners have both aesthetic and practical aims. You might wish to beautify your yard with luxuriant shrub borders and flowerbeds. Your dream might be a vegetable and herb garden or even a backyard orchard. Or you may need a home for special collections of roses, hostas, or daylilies.

Beauty and functionality also can be incorporated into garden structures, some of which can serve dual purposes, such as elevated decks with storage underneath. Well-designed work areas, terraces, fences, and walks will ultimately increase the value of your home.

But before doing anything, think about how much upkeep you're willing to undertake. Spacious lawns, swimming pools, clipped hedges, and rose and vegetable gardens all need considerable maintenance. An automatic irrigation system can save many hours of hand-watering, but there's no way to automate raking, mowing, fertilizing, pruning, and spraying.

GETTING YOUR PLAN ON PAPER

When planning a landscape, first consider sitting areas, recreation areas, and pathways. The prominence of these three (and the materials from which they are made) will depend on the size of the space you have, as well as your wants and needs.

For instance, if you have children, more space may be allocated to recreation. If you are an empty nester or your children are older, you may designate more space for sitting and relaxing. Perhaps your lot is large or a challenge to navigate. In that case, you may allow plenty of room for pathways.

Base Plan

Using the base plan you created (see page 11), sketch these areas onto tracing paper you've laid on top of the plan. The fun begins when you try to fit everything you want into your landscape. Try not to think about positioning specific plants yet. Instead, concentrate on getting general areas onto the plan.

At first, it won't seem possible to include everything you want. Sunny spots are at a premium, but don't be tempted to reduce the size of your sitting area. Keep doodling on more overlays of tracing paper until you find a solution that keeps that space intact. Look for innovative space savers, and think about capitalizing on underused areas. For instance, fruit trees can be espaliered on a fence, and a pond might become a series of large water pots around the garden.

Don't forget to check the connections between the house and the yard. Will the views from the doors and windows lure you outside? Are the house exits connected to the outdoors with comfortably wide paths, a deck, or a small patio? A yard that seems separate from the house won't be used very often.

The simplest garden plans are usually the most effective: a straight path through two or more garden spaces to a focal point, such as a tall urn or a water feature, or a circular path around the lawn, with places to stop along the way. To establish a stronger sense of unity, designers often repeat a shape throughout a landscape: rectangular deck, rectangular pond; circular pond, semicircular seat; diagonal path, diagonal pattern on the fence or diamond-shaped pots. The shape may be taken from the lines of the house— bay windows, for example, might suggest a pattern of ovals.

WHAT YOU WANT

IT'S TIME TO TURN YOUR FOCUS back to what you need and want your outdoor space to become.

Think about how you and your family spend time outdoors. Do you like to entertain? Do your children need a dry play area? Do you want to create a poolside place for relaxing? We've touched on many of these questions earlier in this book, and with good reason: Your answers are the all-important first step to a landscape plan that meets your family's specific needs. The plan may include amenities such as seating, lighting, and storage areas.

ENTERTAINING

Sooner or later almost everyone needs a deck or patio for a party. If you entertain often, you'll want to make sure it is large enough to handle groups comfortably.

How much seating will you need? Visualize where you might place outdoor furniture. Built-in benches are easy to include if you think of them before you begin construction. Decide where to position them to allow for easy conversation, putting people face to face. For evening entertaining, think about installing outdoor lighting; it makes a deck safer and more inviting for use after dark.

If you like to eat outdoors, make sure you allow space to accommodate a table and chairs (a 12-foot square is usually adequate for a table and four chairs). You might want to include a table and benches in your construction plan. Consider the accessibility of the kitchen to the deck. If a wall separates the two, adding a door or a service window could make it easier to move food outdoors.

Plan a place for a barbecue grill. This should be an out-of-the-way spot where no one will bump into the grill, and where smoke won't be a nuisance.

ABOVE: Terraced beds, containers, and accessories transform this hillside into a pleasant place to stroll. RIGHT: Carefully planned fences and plantings lend a sense of privacy to this backyard.

SWIMMING AND SUNNING

When the focus of outdoor living is a swimming pool, the setting can be formal and rectangular or more natural, with the pool's form integrated within an informal landscape. A dining area, a shade-creating roof, or a spa are all delightful extras. You might also consider including sunbathing platforms.

PLANTINGS

Wooden planters can be worked into most garden designs. Just be sure to allow for proper drainage. Deck construction often covers up outdoor faucets; move these before you begin building. You might want to consider installing an automatic irrigation system.

WORK AND STORAGE

No matter how you will use your garden, you'll always value storage space. Where will you put the hose

CLOCKWISE FROM LEFT: A pool needn't be all concrete. This sheltered porch makes an elegant dining room. Twin storage sheds flank an arbor.

and other garden tools or children's play equipment? Where will the outdoor furniture go in bad weather?

On a sloping property, the most obvious place for storage is underneath a deck, where waterproof closets or shelves can be built easily, using the deck's foundation for support. Conceal such storage by skirting the deck with lattice panels. You also can build lift-top benches, and incorporate closets into the design of stairways.

VIEWS

Changing your yard will also change views, both in and out. For instance, building an elevated deck can expose as many unpleasant views as it does attractive ones. Try moving a ladder around and standing on it at the approximate height of your future deck. What can you see? And who can see you? If you value privacy, or if your new view is unsightly, plan to add screens or landscaping to remedy the problem.

SPACE, PRIVACY, PLAY, AND WATER

Because you are now comfortable with the planning process, consider some of the most common problems that homeowners deal with—and some of the solutions they have devised. Too little space and not enough privacy are common complaints. If you have kids, be sure to include a place for them to play outside. Many homeowners now appreciate the great benefit of a water feature in a landscape.

Limited Space

More and more new developments are being built with small yards. Whether from a need to fit ever more houses into ever less space, or to provide options for those looking to downsize, these small spaces don't always exactly resonate with possibilities.

Small gardens need focal points even more than larger ones do, because they have no sweeping vistas. And small spaces can be exciting. Picture an outdoor living room, a dynamic water feature, multiple conversation areas, and tons of lush, tropical ambience. Believe it or not, you can turn this vision into reality and fit all of these features into a 600-square-foot space.

Take special care with the finishing touches. That's where you can indulge in the luxurious or add a touch of whimsy.

For maximum greenery, use lots of climbing vines, such as violet trumpet vine, bougainvillea, or Carolina jessamine. In this way, a small backyard can be transformed into a wonderful, unique living space.

FAR LEFT AND ABOVE: Creating a series of intriguing spaces is simple when you use beds, borders, flagstone paths, and planters. LEFT: Fool the eye with an imaginative painting on your garden wall or door. BELOW: Visually extend your garden space with a generous shrubbery window.

SMALL SPACE DESIGN TIPS

Creating outdoor living areas is the same whether you have a large or compact space. But limited space sharpens the focus and leaves less margin for error. Here's a checklist of design techniques that are particularly effective in small spaces.

• **Create a series of spaces.** Divide the garden into smaller "rooms," using seat walls or hedges.

• **Use mirrors.** In the right place, a mirror or gazing ball can reflect paths and plants, so that the garden seems to go on without end.

• **Extend the garden with a painting.** Painted on a wall, an open gate or an expanse of blooms can create the illusion of spaces beyond.

• **Build a reflecting pool.** Sky and plants mirrored in water can make a garden look larger.

• **Emphasize diagonal lines.** Paving set on the diagonal, or an angled deck or patio, can make a garden seem deeper than it really is.

• **Change levels.** Berms (mounds) and swales (depressions) visually expand outdoor living spaces, as do sunken or raised patios.

• **Conceal part of the garden.** Make it seem larger by hiding the property line with dense shrubbery and by screening parts of the garden from view. Revealing the garden a section at a time adds mystery and anticipation to the space.

• **Borrow scenery.** Incorporate views beyond the borders of your garden into the design. Prune trees to frame a view. Or mound shrubs together to echo distant hills.

• **Play with perspective.** To create the feeling of depth, place large rocks and plants in the foreground, smaller ones in back.

• **Play with color.** Dark foliage recedes, light foliage is prominent. A backdrop of dark conifers seen through white birch trunks, for example, creates the illusion of depth.

• **Visually merge outdoors with indoors.** Using the same flooring in a living room, loggia, or family room and on an adjoining patio, with French doors between them, is one way to visually extend the garden.

• **Don't forget details.** Viewing a small garden is like looking into the heart of a flower: The smallest details loom large. Make every one count. A large terra-cotta pot can contain a whole garden—annuals, perennials, and a shrub—in miniature.

RIGHT: Trees, shrubs, and an umbrella make for an intimate dining area.
BELOW: A pond and tropical plants give this narrow space an exotic feel.
BOTTOM: An adobe wall and rustic door invite guests into the garden.

Privacy

For most people, privacy is an increasingly valuable commodity. Noisy streets, barking dogs, and bright lights shining through bedroom windows at night are just some of the intrusions brought about by houses built close together or located near roadways.

Fortunately, most privacy problems can be solved with creative landscaping. Well-positioned hedges, fences, or walls can shield your house from the street or from neighbors. A tree or an arbor can block the view of your property from the hillside above.

A combination of walls or berms, plants, and a fountain or other water feature can often subdue the noise of a busy nearby street.

In addition to shielding you from the outside world, creating privacy has some extra benefits. Walls and berms, carefully placed, can create outdoor "rooms" and add interest to the garden.

Before you can create privacy, you must determine exactly what you want to block out or shield. Walk around your property at different times of day, identifying sources of noise and areas that require covers or screens. Also evaluate how plantings and additional structures will affect the patterns of sun and shade in your garden. Are there any views you want to preserve? Consider as well how your neighbors will be affected.

A particularly annoying privacy problem might seem to call for a stand of fast-growing, closely spaced trees or shrubs. But don't overdo it. You may end up replacing or removing such plants, because fast growers often are not long-lived. You can, however, plan for selective removal, such as every other shrub in a closely spaced hedge. Or combine both fast- and slow-growing plants, knowing that you'll remove the less desirable ones as the better species mature.

ABOVE: Stepped fencing with lattice provides interest as well as privacy; it also blends well with the home and its surroundings. LEFT: A secluded spot in the garden can be home to a chair surrounded by container plants. BELOW: A pretty line of blooming roses shields the yard from sights and sounds.

Play Areas

Kids love the outdoors and need a place to expend their energy. Yet young children (and some older ones) have little sense of danger, so play areas must be safe as well as fun. The first decision to make when planning such an area is where to place it. Preschoolers feel safer—and can be more easily watched—if the designated space is close to the house. You may prefer to corral older, noisier children farther away but still within view.

Also take into account sun, wind, and shade. Abundant sunlight increases the risk of sunburn and can make metal slides or bars, as well as concrete walks, burning hot, so install slide surfaces facing north. If your property is in the path of frequent strong winds, locate the play area inside a windbreak of fencing or dense trees. Dappled shade is ideal. If you have no spreading foliage, position the play area on the north side of your house and construct a simple lath roof or plastic tarp canopy, or plan a play structure that includes a shaded portion.

Many public playgrounds feature metal play structures rather than timber, because wood may eventually rot and break. Still, wood is a warm and friendly material, and probably a good-quality wooden structure will last as long as your children will want to use it.

Some timbers used in play structures are pressure treated with a chemical preservative, especially if they'll be buried underground. Though the Environmental Protection Agency considers these chemicals safe in regulated amounts, check the kind of preservative used before purchasing or building a play structure, and consider alternatives, such as rot-resistant cedar or redwood. (For information on

landscape lumber, see pages 44-45.)

Some structures allow you to add or change components as your child grows. Play structures are available that you can assemble yourself. Before you buy, try to view an assembled structure and talk with the owners to evaluate its safety and design. Look through the instructions beforehand to be sure you can carry out the assembly.

Allow at least 6 feet of space around all sides of swings, slides, and climbing structures for a fall zone, then cushion it well. A 3-inch

layer of wood chips is one choice; increase the depth to 6 inches under a swing. Shredded bark holds up well, even in windy areas or on slopes. Use ¾- to 1-inch particles of Douglas or white fir bark.

Sand provides another safe landing for falls. For children, the more sand, the better—even a depth of 12 inches is not too much. Building a low wall around a play area will help to contain loose materials, keeping the cushion thick and reducing the cost of replenishing.

LEFT: A fabulous play area can be created from a variety of materials. Basic planks and wood accessories form a sturdy structure for climbing. ABOVE: Bean poles joined by twine become a little house when plants are trained along them. BELOW: Logs and boulders provide seats for playing in the sand.

Turf grass also can serve as a functional play surface. (But avoid mixtures that contain clover, as its flowers attract bees.) Cut grass to a height of about 2 inches for maximum cushioning effect, and make sure to keep sticks and other fallen debris out of the area.

Most children fall in love with anything on wheels. For tricycle wheels, plan a smooth, flat concrete path at least 24 inches wide, preferably as wide as 4 feet. Avoid installing a gravel path, as these often prove frustrating for little ones on vehicles, as well as for very young walkers.

Securely fence the play area from the driveway, as well as from the pool, spa, pond, or any other body of water. You also should fence off sharp tools, garden supplies, and garbage cans. For more on play areas, see page 52.

Ponds and Fountains

It doesn't take much water to soothe the soul, and even the smallest pond can have a cooling effect on an outdoor living area. The size of your pond will be restricted by the space available, but its shape and style are limited only by your imagination. If you wish to start small, consider the portable decorative pools available for purchase, or create your own tub version.

Large traditional ponds of brick, concrete, fitted stone, or tile can blend as easily into contemporary gardens as formal ones. They present the opportunity to introduce color and texture with aquatic plants such as water lilies and floating hyacinths. A raised pond with brick walls provides a classic home for goldfish and koi.

Water features fall into one of three categories: spray fountains, waterfalls, and spill fountains. Spray fountains are most suitable for formal water features, while waterfalls and spill fountains are more casual and require less space.

The obvious spot for a pond is where everyone can enjoy it. But because children find ponds irresistible, the safest locations are in fenced backyards. Check local building codes to learn about any requirements for fencing with self-latching gates, as well as setbacks from property lines, electrical circuits for pumps and lights, and pond depth. Generally, ponds that are less than 24 inches deep do not need a building permit.

If you are planning to add plants or fish to your pond, first consider the conditions in your yard. The pond must be protected from wind and situated away from deciduous trees that shed a steady supply of leaves and twigs into the water. Proper drainage is also important; don't choose a low-lying bottom area that will constantly overflow in wet weather.

Remember that the backyard need not be the only place for a pond. The addition of moving water to a front patio or entryway both cools the air and blocks the noise of passing traffic.

Often it's the border that unifies the pond with the surrounding landscape. There are many choices. Among them: a grass lawn; an adjoining bog garden or rock garden (often piled against a partially raised pond or used at one end of

an inclined site); native stones and boulders; flagstones laid in mortar; a wide concrete lip (especially useful as a mowing strip if grass adjoins the area); brick laid in sand or mortar; redwood or other decay-resistant wood laid as rounds or upright columns; terra-cotta tiles; or railroad ties.

You can find flexible pond liners at Lowe's. Although PVC plastic is the standard material, it becomes brittle with exposure to the sun. More UV-resistant—and twice as expensive—are industrial-grade PVC and butyl-rubber liners. Some pool builders prefer EPDM, a roofing material, available in 10- to 40-foot-wide rolls. Most liners can be cut and solvent-welded to create water features of almost any desired size or shape.

Another option is a preformed fiberglass pool shell, available in different shapes and sizes. They cost more than PVC-lined pools, but last longer—up to 20 years.

MOVING FROM PLANNING TO ACTION

YOU'RE READY TO BEGIN putting it all together. You've measured and gauged, thought and talked, doodled and sketched. Some examples of home landscapes may give you that final push to action.

REMODELED ENTRY

Imagine house hunting one weekend and driving by this home as it used to look. You likely wouldn't even have slowed the car. But a few inexpensive changes gave this dull front yard and entryway a bright new beginning.

The original awning was too low and obscured the door. Replacing it

with a bubble awning made of jet black canvas increased the front door's prominence and helped tone down the high, blank gable. The owner also painted the door a different color than the steps and added a new brass knocker, kick plate, and mail slot.

A lattice trellis on one side of the door helps balance the asymmetrical

BEFORE

facade. Small spacers keep the lattice from touching its black backing, leaving enough room for vines to twine through.

The owner installed a landing at the foot of the steps, using 18-inch-square concrete pads set atop a bed of crushed limestone. Staining every other square black creates a striking checkerboard pattern.

LEFT: Before any demolition takes place, identify the problems you want to address with appropriate solutions. ABOVE: Simple items, such as an awning, a lattice trellis, and some paint transformed this entryway.

A simple planting adds color and minimizes maintenance. After pruning the existing nandinas in a stair-step fashion, the owner framed the entryway with Japanese hollies, ornamental grasses, Southern shield ferns, and a mixture of colorful annuals and perennials. A new 'Natchez' crepe myrtle gives some privacy to the triple front window.

GARDEN REMODELING TIPS

Plan what to keep. If money's no object, you can start over with new structures, such as walls. If you're on a tight budget, consider altering the existing ones or camouflaging them with plants. Large trees are probably worth keeping if they're healthy and can be assimilated into the new design. You may be able to relocate them; a designer or arborist can help you make that decision.

Consider grade changes. Use raised beds or berms, a sunken patio, or seat walls to alter a flat garden.

Choose materials to tie in with the house. A warm-colored house, for instance, calls for warm-colored flagstone.

Give important elements the highest priority. Put your money into structural elements (paths, decks) and slow-growing specimen plants first. You can then save money when buying smaller, less important shrubs, perennials, and ground covers.

REMODELED BACKYARD

When a landscape architect originally looked at this backyard, she envisioned a design in the shape of a four-leaf clover. Her inspiration transformed a barren backyard into a relaxing spot to entertain or simply unwind.

The new clover-shaped terrace is a private nook, separated from neighbors by a fence and screened from the drive by two yaupon hollies that will grow into small gray-barked trees.

One "leaf," or arc, of the terrace provides generous footing for a roomy swing. With night lighting and outdoor stereo speakers nearby, the swing is a perfect place to start or end the day. Another arc leads through the pair of yaupon hollies to the back door. Even though you can see between the slender trunks, the hollies give a sense of separation that makes the area feel secluded. A third arc curves toward the house and creates a spot for a favorite chair as well as a generous planting bed for evergreen shrubs and seasonal flowers. Impatiens edge the terrace throughout the summer.

While the first three arcs have a raised brick edging, the edge of the fourth is paved even with the lawn and invites a stroll.

THE MAKEOVER

Problem: The backyard didn't offer a comfortable place to relax.
Solution: A clover-shaped terrace creates a garden "room" to enjoy.

Problem: Nothing separated the drive from the lawn.
Solution: Yaupon hollies screen the drive from the new terrace.

Problem: Sparse, drab plantings didn't offer seasonal color.
Solution: Beds flanking the terrace accommodate lush evergreens and colorful annuals and perennials.

With no points of interest to begin with, this backyard found new life with pavers in a four-leaf clover pattern, new furniture, and lush plantings.

BEFORE

Diligent planning and hard work turned this boring backyard into a beautiful spot for entertaining and relaxing.

THEY DID IT THEMSELVES

You don't need a big budget to make a big difference. As the owners of this modest older home discovered, all you need are an honest assessment of your property's weaknesses and a game plan for achieving your goals.

In this case, the backyard suffered from some glaring problems. The yard was devoid of interest and bordered by unattractive fences. A sunken flagstone terrace by the door

LEFT: Salvaged flagstones were used to make a durable edging for the new garden beds and parking court. BELOW: The old back steps were torn out and replaced with a generous deck, complete with built-in benches.

was not only too small, but it also drained poorly. To get to the backyard, guests had to leave their cars sandwiched on a narrow flagstone driveway between the owners' house and the one next door.

The Fix

The first order of business was tearing up the old driveway and terrace and stockpiling the stones for later use. Next, contractors removed the flimsy back steps and replaced them

with a deck. Built-in benches on the edges of the deck supply ample seating. A PVC pipe running from a corner downspout under the deck to the side of the house improves drainage. Beside the deck, a service area surrounded by fencing provides hidden storage for garbage cans.

The second phase involved extending the driveway around a large oak, so that it ends with a spacious parking court. Compacted limestone gravel provides a firm

surface. Salvaged flagstones from the old driveway and terrace supplied sturdy edging for the parking court and garden beds, new stone steps leading down from the parking area to the deck, and a new stone terrace in front of the rear bedroom. Beds of shrubs hide existing fences. A new roof and gutters and cosmetic improvements to the house—including fresh paint and shutters for the bedroom window—add the finishing touches.

MAKE IT HAPPEN

I T NEVER FAILS. Guide someone through a beautiful garden, then show them a "before" photo of the site. The first word they always say is "Wow!"

As you look at the projects and ideas on the following pages, you'll be saying "wow" a lot. We have two remarkable before-and-after garden stories to share what great work your neighbors have done. Budgets for these projects can range from quite modest to very large. But if your neighbors can do it, so can you.

These gardens and building projects cover a wide range of subjects, such as building a deck, patio, porch, and play area. Then, beginning on page 66, are ideas for using plants. In each case, note that success depends on attending to structures first and plantings last, based on a comprehensive step-by-step plan.

But a garden's personality doesn't come from plants and structures alone. Much depends on the gardener's knack for adding finishing touches: a glowing copper lantern, a bright glazed pot, a collection of folk art birdhouses. Picture a weathered teak bench nestled among old-fashioned roses or a hammock in the shaded corner of a rustic wooden deck.

Luckily, garden accessories have never been as plentiful and as varied as they are today. Furniture is available in various styles—from English to Grecian to mission. Umbrellas come fitted with lights or with canvas walls that block the wind. Outdoor galleries sell everything from leaf-shaped pavers to giant metal flowers.

STRUCTURES

decks

There's no question that outdoor living is more popular than ever. Creating outdoor "rooms" affords unlimited options for the functions of the space while enhancing enjoyment of the outdoors. A backyard deck can incorporate a range of components, including built-in seating, planters, unique storage spaces, and architectural features, making it an attractive addition to your home.

Whether you use an architect and contractor or decide to build the deck yourself, take your time. It can't be stressed enough that planning is the single most important element of the project, so don't rush this phase. Evaluating your needs is important because there are many options to consider. It's a good idea to start by writing a wish list of items you want your deck to have.

Planning a New Deck
Decks can serve many functions. They can be used as overflow space when entertaining guests, or they can create a quiet atmosphere for enjoying the sun and a good book. Adding a grill and a table and chairs transforms the space into a great outdoor eating area. Decks also may serve as transition areas, linking the house to the yard. Thinking of ways that your deck will be used can help determine its size, placement, and other characteristics.

When you have a good idea of what you want, consult at least three local contractors for bids on labor and materials. These contractors should be familiar with building codes and permits. If you are constructing the deck yourself, check with your local building inspector about specific regulations that apply to your area.

In this section, we've featured two decks, each of which was carefully planned by the respective homeowners.

For the deck pictured here, the homeowners wanted a space to relax outdoors with their children and room to entertain friends. They also needed to create an entryway to their back door and accommodate a large tree that gave the yard much-needed shade.

They decided on an octagonal shape for some of the deck sections to create a functional outdoor room with an unusual look. They also wanted a dimensional effect, so they lowered the dining level and raised the cooking area. This design provides generous space for dining, as well as perfect placement for the grill. The dining space comfortably holds a table and six chairs. The cooking area easily accommodates a large grill. Its placement above the main level and on the outer reaches of the deck allows any smoke to be carried up and away from the dining area.

For the deck featured on the following pages, the homeowners knew they wanted a larger deck that would provide more space for entertaining. Enlarging the area would provide them with an additional entryway as well, connecting the deck with the door to the master bedroom. With this in mind, they designed an elegant staircase and a landing that leads from the center of the structure to the yard beyond.

Putting It Together
With the lumber and other alternative materials available today, it is

ABOVE: Using octagonal sections and multiple levels, this family created a roomy outdoor living area. RIGHT: A raised cooking area allows smoke to be carried up and away from guests. BELOW, RIGHT: Protective copper post caps give the deck a finished look.

easy to incorporate many creative features into your new deck's design. To make it a comfortable space that can accommodate a number of guests or family members, consider some built-in seating (which can also serve as hidden storage), plenty of furniture, and a screened gazebo.

Lattice is an inexpensive way to achieve a dressy effect in outdoor areas. Purchased panels can be positioned to enclose the bottom of a deck. Lattice can also be used to provide shade and privacy, while allowing the air to circulate freely. Train climbing vines to grow across it to add a soft and natural accent.

BEFORE

Herringbone Stairs

Copper Post Caps

Lattice and Lighting

ABOVE, LEFT: A herringbone pattern dresses up stairs designed with a generous 14-inch tread. ABOVE: This portion of the deck comfortably holds a table and umbrella for outdoor dining. A screened gazebo with a ceiling fan provides a shaded, insect-free spot for relaxing. LEFT: Low-intensity lighting makes it possible to enjoy time on the deck into the evening.

Decorating the Great Outdoors

Once the structure was complete, the owners set out to decorate their new outdoor space. The selected furniture provides the family with sturdy pieces that are lightweight enough to be moved from one part of the deck to another. This furniture is attractive and easy to maintain because of its rust-free aluminum frames. A large round table and lots of chairs give the family space to dine outdoors. Love seats and side tables also make it easy to relax in the shade. Water-resistant cushions snap onto the chairs, and a market umbrella cranks up easily for protection from sun or light rain. Terra-

cotta pots filled with ferns provide a soft finishing touch to the deck's overall look.

The project that began with plenty of patient thought and careful planning ended with a beautiful deck, and this family has been reaping the benefits ever since.

TOP, RIGHT: Blooming potted plants, lightweight furniture, and other accessories furnish this outdoor room.
ABOVE, LEFT AND RIGHT: A large deck, anchored with a low brick wall and stone-bordered natural area, gives the backyard—and the back of the house—a whole new look. Rails and a roomier staircase make the space user-friendly.

It's no secret that getting the job done right is much easier when you have the proper tools. Here are a few that were helpful in building the decks on these pages.

Table saw—This saw makes short work of cutting all the angles necessary for the herringbone design, as well as borders around deck sections.

Nail gun with compressor—This handy tool makes it easy to drive and countersink a lot of nails, leaving no marks on your lumber.

Miter saw—Angled cuts necessary for ceiling joists, floor joists, and staircase spindles are much easier thanks to this saw.

Power auger—Every well-made deck starts with concrete footings. Do your back and shoulders a favor, and rent a power auger to dig these holes.

Concrete mixer—Here's another rental tool that will save you a lot of time and effort. If you have more than four footings to pour, consider renting one of these.

Water level—This handy tool allows you to level parts that are far apart, such as the ledger board and support posts.

Post level—This device is a special wraparound level that attaches to a post and allows you to plumb it in both directions at the same time.

LEFT: Built-in benches also serve as storage bins for gardening supplies and other items. **BELOW:** Roomy steps flanked by potted plants give a side entrance an elegant feel. The power meter is disguised by a clever cabinet.

Shop Smart: Lumber

Your choice in lumber, which will take the biggest bite out of your project budget, strongly influences the appearance of your deck. It pays to explore the options carefully before you make a final plan.

Softwood or hardwood? All woods are one or the other. The terms don't refer to a wood's relative hardness, but to the kind of tree from which it comes. Softwoods come from evergreens (conifers), hardwoods from broad-leafed (deciduous) trees. Decks are generally built from softwoods, which are less expensive. However, more economical offerings of traditionally high-end hardwoods such as mahogany, angico, and plantation-grown teak have entered the market recently.

Heartwood and Sapwood: A wood's properties are determined by the part of the tree from which it came. The inactive wood nearest the center of a living tree is called heart-

Composite lumber is available in ready-made parts to give your deck a professional look.

Choose the type and grade of wood for your project based on suitability for its intended use; don't scrimp or overbuild.

wood. Sapwood, which is next to the bark, contains the growth cells. Heartwood is more resistant to decay; sapwood is more porous and absorbs preservatives and other chemicals more efficiently.

Among heartwoods, the most decay-resistant and termite-proof species are redwood and cedar. This durability, combined with their natural beauty, makes them favorites for decking. On the other hand, they are softer, weaker, and more expensive than ordinary structural woods such as Douglas fir and Southern pine. To get the best of both worlds, professionals use fir or another structural wood for substructures and redwood or cedar for parts of the project that show. For any wood within 6 inches of the ground or concrete foundations, however, choose a decay-resistant material such as heartwood or sealed sapwood.

Grades: Lumber is sorted and graded at the mill. Generally, lumber grades represent several factors: natural growth characteristics (such as knots); defects resulting from milling errors; and commercial drying and preserving treatments that affect strength, durability, and appearance. The higher the grade of the lumber, the

better the wood—and the more you will have to pay for it.

Redwood is usually graded for its appearance and for the percentage of heartwood versus sapwood it contains. Among pure heartwoods, Clear All Heart is the very best grade, then B Heart, Construction Heart, and Merchantable Heart, in descending order.

Cedar grades, starting with the highest quality, are Architect Clear, Architect Knotty, and Custom Knotty. These grades don't indicate heartwood or sapwood.

Treated Lumber: Though redwood and cedar heartwoods resist decay and termites, other woods that come in contact with the ground or trap water may quickly rot and lose their strength. For this reason, less durable types such as Southern pine and Western hem/fir (a commercial designation for wood of Western hemlock or fir) are often factory treated with preservatives to protect them from rot, insects, and other sources of decay. These woods are generally less expensive and in many areas more readily available than redwood or cedar. They can be used for surface decking as well as for structural members such as posts, beams, and joists.

Working with treated lumber can be difficult. Compared with redwood and cedar, which are easy

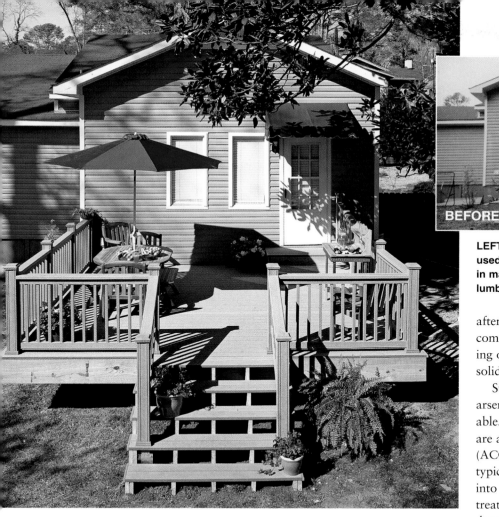

BEFORE

LEFT: The composite decking material used to create this deck was available in many pieces you might find in the lumberyard—boards, posts, and rails.

to cut and nail or screw, treated wood is often hard and brittle and is more likely to warp or twist. In addition, some people object to its typically greenish brown color (apply a stain to conceal it) and the staple-like incisions that usually cover it (some types come without these marks).

Because the primary preservative used contains chromium and arsenic (both toxic chemicals), you should wear safety glasses and a dust mask when cutting treated lumber, and you should never burn it.

Even arsenic-free pressure-treated wood still needs to be handled with care. That includes washing hands

after touching it, not letting food come in contact with it, and disposing of wood according to local solid-waste requirements.

Substitutes for chromated copper arsenate (CCA) are already available. The two main replacements are alkaline copper quaternary (ACQ) and copper azote, both typically injected under pressure into Southern yellow pine. Wood treated with either is as resistant to decay and termites as wood treated with CCA.

Lumber Alternatives: When it comes to lumber, you might consider woods other than the best grades of redwood and cedar, which generally come from the oldest trees. Instead, seek out plantation-grown woods or those from certified forests; or look for suppliers of salvaged lumber from orchards or demolished buildings.

Plastic-and-wood composites and all-plastic products also resist rot and insects, as well as the sun's ravages. While good for decking and railings, these options don't have the strength of wood and are currently not available in the larger dimensions needed to frame decks; for that, there is plastic structural lumber. These nonwood alternatives generally are priced competitively with the higher grades of redwood and cedar.

HANDLING CCA-TREATED WOOD

Here are guidelines regarding proper handling of lumber that has been pressure-treated with chemical preservatives.

● Never burn it in open fires, stoves, fireplaces, or residential boilers.

● Never recycle it for mulch or compost.

● Wear a dust mask when sawing or sanding it. Wear gloves when working it, and wash skin exposed to it before eating or drinking.

● Do not allow food to come into direct contact with any treated wood or adjacent soil.

BEFORE

Interlocking pavers and a stucco wall help create a retreat for these homeowners. Pavers come in a variety of shapes, colors, and materials. Whether you use flagstone or basic brick, you can incorporate a multitude of shapes and curves in your patio's design.

patios

Patio Planning

The first step in planning a patio is—at the risk of sounding like a broken record—to focus clearly on your family's needs and habits. Think about the way you spend your leisure time. Consider your lifestyle. If you frequently entertain outdoors, do you prefer casual or formal gatherings? How much time do you want to spend gardening and maintaining your yard? Do you have pets that may damage fragile patio plants and furniture? Your answers to these questions will help to determine some basic design elements for your patio.

Next, evaluate your yard's assets and liabilities. Even if you plan to enlist the services of a landscape architect or other professional, you need to have a good understanding of your existing landscape. Can the patio take advantage of a beautiful view? Is your property bounded by woods? Perhaps the design can capitalize on a sunny southern

exposure, mature plantings, or one distinctive element—such as an attractive tree.

Also consider potential handicaps. Is your lot on a steep slope? How much of the lot is exposed to street traffic and noise? Does your present patio open off the wrong room, get too much sun or shade, or lack sufficient space? You'll want to plan a patio that minimizes your yard's special problems.

The patio's exact location will depend largely on the size and contour of your lot, the way your house is sited, your preferred uses for the patio, and your climate.

Patio Paver Essentials

The average patio hosts a wide variety of outdoor activities. With the right amenities, it can be a breakfast nook, living area, reading room, and play area all in one. Before you get to the stage of choosing amenities, however, you'll want to select the patio's more basic elements: its surface material, edging, and any stairs or walkways required to join the patio to the garden or to link different areas. Your decisions about these essentials will determine the style and cost of your project.

With careful preparation and installation, a brick-in-sand path or patio will be as durable as bricks set in mortar. Also, if you decide to change the surface later, you need only to chip out one brick to remove the rest in perfect condition.

Typically, you prepare a bed of 1½- to 2-inch-thick sand or rock fines (a mix of grain sizes) and lay the bricks compactly, with no spaces between. If the drainage is poor, you may need to first lay a 4-inch gravel base (in areas where the ground freezes, 6 to 8 inches is advisable). A layer of landscape fabric will suppress the growth of weeds.

To hold both the bricks and sand firmly in place, first build permanent edgings around the perimeter; they serve as good leveling guides for preparing and laying the bricks. If you have to do a lot of cutting or shaping of complex angles (along curved edgings, for example), rent a brick saw from a masonry supplier or tool rental outlet.

Concrete pavers can also be laid in sand, much like bricks. With

interlocking types, alignment is nearly automatic. After laying these units, make several passes with a power-plate vibrator to tamp soil. You can probably rent a vibrator locally; if not, use a heavy drum roller instead. Spread damp fine sand over the surface; when it dries, sweep it into the paver joints. Additional passes with either a vibrator or roller will help lock the pavers together.

LEFT: When planning your patio, try to incorporate decorative elements, such as this built-in planter. BELOW: Simple bricks transformed this backyard into a roomy, functional spot for relaxing and entertaining.

BEFORE

a paver project

From the moment they step into the yard, visitors are welcomed by this easy-to-make walkway. Pavers allow you to create different looks through patterns and colors, and they blend in well with the landscape. At the end of the walk, a simple arbor frames the entryway stairs.

The original entrance to this house was plain and almost inaccessible, with a small brick landing bordered by old, rotted railroad ties at the bottom of the steps. It made the front yard and house seem gloomy.

The homeowner wanted a simple yet unique way to enliven his entrance. He removed the old bricks and railroad ties and dug up the soil to make space for a new walkway. Using multicolored pavers, crushed stone, and some scrap wood and tin, he turned his hard-to-spot front entry into an inviting haven. Now his visitors are drawn in from the driveway by the patterned walk and the enticing arbor at the bottom of the steps.

Here's How

Step 1: Use 1 yard of crushed stone as a base to level the pavers. Crushed stone is a good choice because it won't sift away like sand. And unlike easily tunneled sand, the sharp edges of crushed stone are difficult for chipmunks and moles to burrow through. Use a 2 x 4 or a scrap of lumber to smooth the gravel along the walkway.

Step 2: Set the pavers on top of the crushed stone. Align 10 square pavers to create a diamond pattern

ABOVE: A paver pathway set with crushed stone transitions smoothly to a nearby concrete pad. LEFT: Using only two basic pavers—square and rectangular—this homeowner created an interesting pattern.

in the center of the walk. Use rectangular pavers in a different color to edge the diamonds, alternating the direction that the rectangular pavers are laid from one diamond to the next. (See photo on page 48.)

Step 3: Fill the triangular spaces left between the pavers and the edge of the driveway with excess crushed stone. Sweep stone into the gaps between the pavers to help set them.

Step 4: Water the crushed stone to work it into the cracks and create a hard-packed surface.

Step 5: On the other side of the pavers, fill the spaces with topsoil to create planting pockets. For a great kick of color in the fall, plant mums. Planting the flowers while they are tightly budded and not showing color will provide a lengthy bloom along the walkway. **Tip:** This homeowner took existing shrubs and ferns from his yard and incorporated them around the mums. Make the most of existing plants to save money.

Step 6: Weather the walkway by using a concrete-aging product on the pavers, if desired.

Lowe's Creative Ideas for Outdoor Living **49**

BEFORE

ABOVE: This porch addition changed the look of the home and enhanced the space where the family can spend time outdoors. RIGHT: Flagstone steps, a weighty column, and plenty of potted plants give this entry a balanced look.

BEFORE

porches

Power to the Porch

A porch with attractive plantings that enhance your house's curb appeal is one of the best investments you can make. Yet for most homeowners, the front yard is far from ideal. It may be a virtual blank slate, with neither personality nor character. Or it may be outdated, with a narrow walkway, basic porch, a ring of shrubs around the foundation, and a concrete slab at the door.

Conversely, your front yard may be so overgrown with foliage that the house is hidden. To transform it, focus first on the entry walkway and porch. Make it so clear and

obvious and generously sized that guests are never confused about the best route to the front door and are always comfortable getting there. Also use materials for the path and driveway that complement and enhance your house's facade.

Almost every house has a porch. The problem is that they are often small, unadorned concrete slabs barely large enough for two people carrying shopping bags. If your porch looks like a construction afterthought, enlarging it and

In each of these photos, screens transform a space into one that can be enjoyed most months of the year for dining or visiting with family and friends. With some careful planning, a screening system can easily be installed on an existing porch or patio.

If your house lacks a front porch or only has a diminutive one, you can build your own. The facade of the house on the opposite page was transformed by the owners with the addition of a front porch. They built it themselves, adapting ideas and techniques as they worked.

Screened Porches

In some regions, enjoyment of outdoor living spaces is limited by insects. In the evening, the same time you want to be outdoors, the mosquitoes come to life. The easiest way to keep bugs at bay is to screen part of your space.

If you're starting from scratch, installing a commercial awning or canopy with screens is probably the easiest and quickest route to a fullfledged screened room. But if you have a roof over your porch (or patio or deck), adding screens is a fairly straightforward task. The easiest method involves installing 1 x 1 strips on the support members of the overhead structure and stapling screening to it. The staples and edges of the screening are then covered with screen bead moulding. The downside to this approach is that the screening is not removable. An alternative is to mount screened frames in the openings.

adding some attractive details will bring your house up to date and provide some much needed space.

That was exactly the case with the porch featured at the top, far left. The original porch was bland, not to mention uninviting, and the landscaping was minimal. The owners strengthened their home's exterior style by adding shutters, lattice panels, and some comfortable wicker furniture on the porch. This created a more inviting entrance while extending the living space to

the outdoors. They also replaced the spindly metal supports with classic Chippendale-style rails and Doric columns.

The special details make this porch a welcoming one. Roomy stairs invite you in, then benches occupy the porch's ample space, allowing plenty of spots for relaxing. Shrubs and small trees, potted plants, hanging baskets, and window boxes all soften the edges of the space and add some much needed color.

play areas

Kid Stuff

As children explore the outdoors through endless hours of play, their delight is obvious. You can hear it in the giggles rippling from the sandbox and see it in the antics on any school playground. And what better place is there for them to take advantage of fresh air and sunshine than your own backyard? Many of the features found in a playground, such as slides and swings, can be built by the do-it-yourselfer with a modicum of ability.

Whether your children are toddlers or school age, you can add outdoor fun to their backyard play area with the ideas shown here. From a beanpole tepee to an elaborate jungle gym or a mobile lemonade stand (see page 124), you'll discover enough inspiration here to turn any backyard into a child's delight.

Sandboxes are a popular play feature. Add a wide rim around the top for a convenient seat. You should also consider including a lid to keep out pets, leaves, and rain. For complete building instructions for the sandbox shown on page 53, see page 110.

And don't forget the family pet. Add a creative doghouse, such as the one shown at right, to complete the play area. See the shopping list, cut list, and assembly diagrams on pages 113-116.

Make sure the structures you build or choose for kids' activities offer plenty of safe, imaginative play, while encouraging varied physical exercise. Swing sets and sand aren't the only things that delight children.

Note: While all the ideas shown here have been tested by parent-builders, there is still a certain element of risk in any playground activity, especially one involving heights, such as a jungle gym. Pay attention to safety tips (see guidelines for handling pressure-treated wood on page 45) and use common sense; remember that children need to be supervised by an adult at all times.

Where Imagination Rules

Perhaps the ultimate embellishment to a play area is a playhouse. Designs range from small-scale Victorian mansions to fairy-tale cottages. If you plan properly, the playhouse can have a second life as a potting shed or a storage area when the kids grow up. Before you begin construction, though, check local building codes—you may need to obtain a permit.

One family decided to encourage their daughter's love of playing school, so they created a playhouse that would be her very own classroom— a place where she could have fun teaching her neighborhood friends

CREATE A CUSTOMIZED HOME FOR YOUR FAMILY PET. TURN TO PAGE 113 FOR INSTRUCTIONS AND PLANS FOR THE DECORATIVE DOGHOUSE SHOWN HERE. THE MOBILE SANDBOX PROJECT BEGINS ON PAGE 110.

and Rose, her pet beagle.

The parents ordered a prefabricated, 8-foot-square wooden shed. An old concrete slab in the backyard was perfect to serve as a site, but they ordered a wooden floor kit to add comfort for the children. It took the parents a weekend to

assemble the building and do the roofing. A cupola was made from scrap treated plywood, and attached to the roof before the shingles were added. The building took on the look of a schoolhouse once it was painted red with off-white trim. The interior walls were primed and

ABOVE, LEFT: A simple slide doesn't need much space. This one was incorporated into an existing slope in the family's garden. Kits available at Lowe's allow for the creation of customized play structures. ABOVE, RIGHT: This cottage playhouse provides room for tea parties and toy storage. Eclectic accessories give it a whimsical look that is easy to change as the kids grow older.

painted the same off-white shade, but in a satin finish. After the inside was painted, an 8-foot piece of indoor/outdoor carpet was installed over the flooring boards.

All materials were delivered pre-cut, and the assembly was just a two-person job using everyday tools found around the house.

Four utility windows were placed on the sides of the shed to provide daylight and ventilation. The last exterior details added were two dummy knobs, a flag, and a bell. Summer school would soon begin.

ABOVE: With some paint and a few additions, this 8- x 8-foot shed becomes a schoolhouse. Storage bins, outdoor containers, and a deacon's bench provide space for toys. BELOW: Casters make this sandbox a mobile play area that is easy to move to a sheltered space during the winter. The lid keeps out debris and doubles as a play surface.

Get little ones outdoors with a garden they help to plant. Kid-sized tools make harvesting more fun than work.

Kids and Gardening

Children love to dig in the dirt, so gardening is a natural outlet for their energy as well as an enjoyable way to spend quality time with them. Give them each a plant or two to care for over the summer, and watch their nurturing nature grow along with their gardens. And why not involve them in some of your gardening jobs, such as pulling weeds or harvesting vegetables for dinner? Gardening will provide many hours of productive summer entertainment for your children.

BEFORE

This room off a poolside patio was transformed into a kid-friendly pool house with easy-to-clean walls and furniture, storage cubbies, and pegs for towels and suits.

VINE-COVERED TEPEE

Kids love to hide out in a leafy tepee, but grown-ups need a bit of coaxing. Be adult about it, we say. Admit you can picture yourself under these leaves—sitting cross-legged, palms up, practicing your mantra per-haps. Or curled up in an Indian blanket, sneaking a snooze. Pick your pleasure. Don't you deserve your own tepee?

This project will take you about an hour and cost about $20. You'll need six 8-foot poles (bamboo or other) that are at least 1 inch thick, about 60 feet of heavy twine, and about 80 feet of clothesline rope. And you'll need seeds of a fast-growing vine.

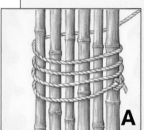

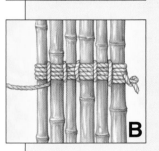

Assembly

Step 1: Line up poles on the ground, alternating thick and thin ends. Pull the second, fourth, and sixth poles to the right, until approximately 2 feet of the six poles overlap in the center.
Step 2: Fasten a 10-foot length of twine to the first pole by tying a sturdy hitch or knot. Loop the twine loosely around all six poles three or four times, allowing some space between poles (A).
Step 3: Secure the loops by binding twine around them at right angles, weaving it between the poles (B). At the final pole, fasten off the binding by tying a hitch or knot.
Step 4: Pick up the poles and spread them in a circle—arranging poles so that the six thin ends cross at the top—to form a tepee with a diameter of about 8 feet. Allow extra space between the two poles that will frame the entrance.

Support Grid

Step 1: String clothesline rope horizontally around the tepee at 1-foot intervals, except at the entrance (C). As you work, wrap the clothesline once around each pole and give it a tug to take up the slack.
Step 2: To complete the grid, attach two or three lengths of twine vertically to the clothesline between pairs of poles.

Planting

Sow seeds directly in well-cultivated soil around the outside circumference of the tepee, except in front of the entrance. Train the vines up the poles and the twine. It takes about two months for the vines to cover the whole tepee.

Hyacinth bean vine *(Dolichos lablab),* a prolific bloomer, covers the tepee shown at right. Also try climbing nas-turtium *(Tropaeolum),* climbing snapdragon *(Asarina),* sweet pea *(Lathyrus odoratus),* or scarlet runner bean *(Phaseolus coccineus),* which bears bright scarlet blooms that develop into tasty shelling beans.

Tepees are favorite hideouts for kids and are easily constructed by parents.

ROSE-DRAPED ARBOR

The first item on the landscape wish list of these homeowners was a secluded area where they could read and relax. To fulfill that wish, they created an arbor that would be shrouded by that grande dame of climbing roses, Lady Banks's *(Rosa banksiae)*.

They worked with a local designer to create a circular arbor about 8 feet high, with a diameter of 16½ feet, composed of tubular steel panels. Around the foot of the arbor, they planted 14 rose plants, alternating yellow-flowered 'Lutea' and white-flowered *R. b. banksiae* 'Alba Plena'. The roses covered the panels and arched over the top, creating an enclosed outdoor room. A 4½-foot-wide gap provides an entrance to the brick-floored room, which is outfitted with wicker furniture.

The homeowners now enjoy shade cast by the canopy of evergreen foliage year-round, and masses of blooms cover the arbor from late February through April. Low-voltage lights at the base of the arbor create a dramatic effect at night.

arbors & gazebos

There's nothing quite like an arbor or gazebo to enhance your enjoyment of the garden. Gazebos can furnish shade during the day and shelter during cool evenings, yet are open to breezes and the enticing scent of flowers. They give you a place to sit and relax, host a party, or simply mingle with family and friends. And arbors play practical roles as well: They can link your house to the garden, define different areas of the yard, direct foot traffic through the landscape, mask an unattractive feature, or frame a spectacular view.

Gazebos come in a variety of styles, from old-fashioned Victorian designs to contemporary or rustic motifs. Though typically built with open, airy framing, a gazebo lends a feeling of enclosure to those sitting within. By contrast, arbors frame the walls and ceiling of an outdoor room and can be embellished with fragrant or colorful vines. You can build an arbor in almost any style, from simple archways to elaborate neoclassical pavilions.

As you think about where to put a new arbor or gazebo, take walking tours of your property under differing weather conditions. Glance back at the house often. Look for a vantage point that marries a good view of the house with the property as a whole. Also consider exposure—if your main deck or patio is in full sun, you may prefer to locate an arbor or gazebo in a shady corner. Lastly, don't give up on a garden structure just because your yard is small. Tiny spaces often profit from the focal point created by a small arbor or gazebo.

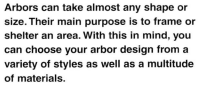

Arbors can take almost any shape or size. Their main purpose is to frame or shelter an area. With this in mind, you can choose your arbor design from a variety of styles as well as a multitude of materials.

WHAT A GREAT IDEA

RUSTIC ARBOR

Sometimes all a sitting area needs to make it more appealing is a simple arbor. Here's one with rustic charm that was built in a day.

The five-sided structure is made from downed branches of madrona, a rot-resistant wood found chiefly on the Pacific coast of North America. First, cut five 8½-foot lengths for the vertical posts, and sink each post 18 inches into the ground. Then, cut large branches to span the uprights, and attach them with 6-inch screws. Finally, top the arbor with small branches and twigs, and wire as many as possible in place to secure them from the wind.

fences

Well-designed fences filter the sun's glare, turn a raging wind into a pleasant breeze, and help muffle the cacophony of street traffic, noisy neighbors, and barking dogs. On the other hand, walls bring an unmatched sense of permanence to a garden. Both function as partitions, dividing the yard into separate areas for recreation, relaxation, gardening, and storage. Although fences serve many of the same purposes as walls, they are generally less formal in appearance, easier to construct, and, when you calculate labor costs, less expensive to build.

Most communities have regulations restricting fence height. In many places, the maximum allowable height is 42 inches for front-yard fences and 6 feet for backyard ones. An alternative way to gain more height is to clothe the top of the fence with a vine or to plant shrubs adjacent to it, and then allow them to grow beyond the height of the fence. Before you begin your construction, check the building codes of your community. Some locales have design covenants that may affect your project.

Occasionally a boundary fence is owned and maintained by both neighbors. Make every effort to come to a friendly agreement with your neighbor on the location, design, and construction of the fence. (One option is a "good neighbor" fence with siding mounted in alternating directions.) If you can't come to an agreement, you can circumvent the problem by building the fence entirely on your property, just a few inches inside your boundary.

Before installing your fence, check the terrain. Few lots are perfectly smooth, flat, and free of

ABOVE: Climbing vines and border plantings soften the angular lines of this fence and entry. BELOW: A fence can be easily adapted to the uneven contours of a hilly or rolling landscape.

obstructions. If your fence line runs up a hill, build the fence so that it follows the contours of the land, or construct stepped panels that will maintain horizontal lines.

Most fences are built entirely of wood. Wood's versatility as a fencing material is reflected in its wide variety—split rails, dimensional lumber, poles, and manufactured wood products such as plywood and tempered hardboard.

Wooden fences normally have three parts: vertical posts, horizontal rails (or stringers), and siding. Posts are usually made of 4 x 4 pine or fir or decay-resistant redwood or cedar heartwood. Redwood and cedar can be left to weather naturally, but fir or pine should be painted or stained. Rails are usually 2 x 4s. Fence siding can vary from pre-assembled picket sections to plywood panels.

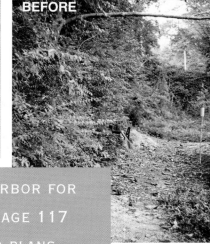

ABOVE, LEFT: Using natural materials helps a fence blend in with its surroundings. ABOVE: Plantings can hide a fence. FAR LEFT: Liven up a fence with a whimsical painting. LEFT AND BELOW: This fence and arbor established boundaries and tamed a wild backyard.

BEFORE

CREATE A FENCE AND ARBOR FOR YOUR YARD. TURN TO PAGE 117 FOR INSTRUCTIONS AND PLANS.

Alternative materials include vinyl, galvanized wire, plastic mesh, and ornamental iron. To soften the look of a wire fence, plant annual vines—such as morning glories or climbing nasturtiums—for quick cover, and add plantings for permanent cover.

Most wooden fences fall into one of three basic types: post-and-rail, picket, or solid board. Your choice will depend on the fence's intended function. A board fence may be the best privacy screen, for example.

To increase seclusion and wind protection, look to a closed design, such as face panel or grape stake fencing. When you want to break up a large expanse—in a solid panel fence, for instance—a simple oval or square window that frames a view lends a sense of mystery and discovery. Shrubs planted along a fence also soften the look of solid fencing.

For some degree of privacy without compromising ventilation, vertical lath (narrow strips of wood) or lattice is a good choice, as long as the space doesn't require complete protection. Vines trained onto lattice trellises or wire frames can block wind and sun without destroying the airy, open feeling of your patio. Louvers, slats, lattice, or see-through trellises provide a glimpse of what lies beyond.

walls

Among the typical materials for garden walls are masonry units or blocks, uncut stone, and poured concrete. The easiest materials for the do-it-yourselfer are brick and concrete block, which are uniform units with modular proportions that you assemble piece by piece. You can choose a decorative pattern for laying the courses, incorporate a solid or openwork face, and vary the thickness. You might even employ combinations of materials.

Regardless of the type of wall you plan to build, you need to support it with a solid foundation or footing. Poured concrete is best, because it can be smoothed and leveled better than other materials. Usually, footings are twice the width of the wall and at least as deep as the wall is wide. But consult local codes for exceptions. For very low walls (no more than 12 inches high) or for low raised beds, you can lay the base of the wall directly on tamped soil or in a leveled trench.

In most cases, a freestanding wall more than 2 or 3 feet high should have reinforcement to tie portions of the wall together and prevent it from collapsing. (Check your local building codes.) Steel reinforcing bars, laid with the mortar along the length of a wall, provide horizontal stiffening. Placed upright (for example, between double rows of brick or within the hollow cores of concrete blocks), reinforcing adds vertical strength that can keep a wall from toppling due to its own weight. Special steel ties in various patterns are made for reinforcing masonry or attaching a stone veneer to a poured-concrete or concrete-block substructure.

Vertical columns of masonry, called pilasters, can be tied into a

CLOCKWISE FROM ABOVE: A garden wall can make your home look more established and enhance its architecture. You can adjust the amount of privacy, light, and air your garden wall permits by using decorative elements such as cutwork, windows and other openings, or glass block.

wall to provide vertical support. Many building codes require that they be used at least every 12 feet. Also consider placing pilasters on either side of an entrance gate and at the ends of freestanding walls.

MAGICAL MAKEOVER

APPLYING VENEER TO A BLOCK WALL

Take advantage of concrete blocks' low cost and speed of assembly to build a wall. Then cover it with plastering stucco for attractive texture and shape. Though plastering is an acquired technique, an accomplished do-it-yourselfer might reasonably tackle a small garden wall.

Plastering a block wall is a two-part operation. The first layer—or "scratch coat"—should be about ⅜ inch thick and can only be applied after you have painted the wall with a concrete bonding agent or covered it with wire lath. Then rough up the scratch coat with a commercial tool to help the finish coat's "bite." Apply the finish coat to a thickness of ¼ inch. When the sheen has dulled, give texture to the plaster's surface by floating on the finish coat with a steel trowel, a sponge, or a stiff brush.

For best results, buy plaster premixed. If the color is integral, consult with your supplier about coloring oxides, and plan to use a mix with white concrete and sand in it.

BIG LOOKS,
simple ideas

STENCIL WALL PAINTINGS

A wide variety of stencils with garden themes can help you embellish outdoor walls with bright images of flowers, vines, pots, or trees. Patterns of twining ivy, wisteria, or even large flower pots are now available through mail-order suppliers (to find suppliers, check the directory sections of home-decorating magazines).

Stencils are usually made of plastic film with a cutout image in the center; you tape them onto the surface you wish to paint with masking tape, then apply paint inside the cutout to create your image. Exterior latex paint—which comes in small cans and many colors—is the best choice for painting stucco or adobe walls.

Start with a clean, dry surface. Apply paint from the outside of the stencil cutout to the center. To enhance plant images, add hand-painted details such as vines, veins, and tendrils.

For crisp images and edges, use a clean, dry stencil brush with a flat top and firm, but not stiff, natural bristles. A sponge works best for creating soft images or textures. On some designs, you may want to alternate between these two techniques.

sheds & storage

It's amazing how quickly gardening supplies pile up. Sooner or later every homeowner has to face the challenge of where they can all be stored. While the garage is often the answer, a gardening shed can be both a practical and handsome solution. If you make it big enough to include a counter surface for potting plants and other tasks, the space will be even more functional.

Place a shed where you can easily get to it—you don't want to hike

TOP: Sheds and other storage structures don't have to be boring and strictly utilitarian. ABOVE: Take a cue from the surroundings to inspire the look of your design, as with this faux ramshackle shed.

across the yard to retrieve a trowel. But if the shed is purely utilitarian, try to nestle it away from outdoor entertainment areas. Fenced yards can often accommodate a small storage space in a corner. Repeating the fence pattern on the surface of

the shed minimizes the impact the structure has on the view.

The easiest route to obtaining additional storage is a prefabricated shed, available at Lowe's in several different styles and sizes. More expensive—but also more attractive—are wood sheds, either built from scratch or constructed from a kit. Although a concrete foundation is preferable for a wood shed, you can cut costs by placing the structure on concrete blocks and building a wooden ramp down to ground level. Check with your local building department before adding a shed; if the building is considered permanent you may need a permit.

How To Organize Sheds

Once the exterior of the shed is complete, tackle the inside. Because the building will be used primarily as a garden shed, potting space is a given, as is storage for gardening tools and supplies. You may also want to store larger lawn equipment from an overflowing garage and perhaps set up a spot for woodworking projects.

In the picture at far right, two 60-inch unfinished cabinets with butcher-block countertops are used to provide a good, durable work surface for both gardening and woodworking. The 36-inch height of the cabinets means no stooping as you work on projects. The cabinets also provide a generous work surface and ample storage for supplies, including large bags of potting soil and fertilizer, gallons of paint, tools, and equipment.

Once the cabinets are in place and secured to the frame of the shed, install 4-foot-square sheets of peg-board on the walls. This functional material lends a finished look to the exposed framing and provides additional storage solutions.

BEFORE

TOP, LEFT AND ABOVE: This once-dilapidated shed was cleaned up and refurbished, creating a functional place for tools and supplies. **TOP, RIGHT AND ABOVE:** Peg-board, cabinets, and countertops add to the utility of the structure. **BELOW:** No matter its size, design your storage space to blend with your home's architecture, and incorporate utility elements, such as pegs for bike and tools and shelves.

WORKBOOK PROJECT

POTTING BENCH

Because furnishings are an important element of a stylish deck or patio and potting benches are so useful, consider incorporating this functional potting bench into your deck. The bench has multilevel storage space and an ample work surface, along with a place to store pots, soil, and other gardening essentials. At a moment's notice, the potting bench can be reworked as a buffet, ready to accommodate friends of all ages.

CREATE THIS VERSATILE POTTING BENCH FOR YOUR DECK. PLANS AND INSTRUCTIONS BEGIN ON PAGE 120.

Once assembled, the bench was covered with an opaque exterior stain to add instant color and to give the wood a weathered appearance. The stain both protects and seals the wood, making it weather resistant.

ABOVE: Roomy potting areas can contain such things as wheelbarrows trash bins, and lots of supplies. LEFT: A small potting bench can be tucked into almost any space, but be sure you have good storage and an adequate work surface.

work centers

If you plan to do any serious gardening, you'll likely find a garden work center to be an invaluable addition to your home.

A work center serves as a central place for storing gardening tools and materials, and also provides table space for potting and other gardening work. The typical features of a garden work center include a potting counter, bins or other containers for fertilizer and potting material, a sink, racks for tools and pots, and shelves for seeds and bottles.

The best garden work centers are planned to meet the needs of the gardener and often must fit into a limited space. While it's possible to adapt a shed to the purpose, working inside a dark building on a sunny day is an unappealing idea for most gardeners. A better plan is using an exterior wall to support a small work center such as the ones shown here.

These work centers are designed to suit a variety of situations. Adapt them to your needs, or let them inspire you to create your own design. Whether intended to be supported by the side of a fence or garage, or to be freestanding, work centers should be located in a convenient yet unobtrusive spot where they won't detract from the larger garden design. A more elaborate work center would incorporate a large screen to conceal the work area from the house and display areas.

ABOVE, LEFT: Many potting benches are available in kit form. ABOVE: Others can be simply constructed from dimensional lumber. A modular sink can be hooked up to an outdoor water supply for rinsing pots and garden tools and filling watering cans.

WHAT A GREAT IDEA

SHUTTER-AWNING PROJECT

Where space is limited, incorporate a work center into your deck. The project shown at left took an awkward space along a chimney and transformed it into a semi-sheltered work area. The homeowner created an awning from shutters mounted 8 feet above the deck, and then placed a sturdy table beneath for potting plants or displaying the week's harvest. Follow these steps to fashion your own shutter awning.

Step 1: Lightly sand unfinished shutters. Spray shutters with primer.

Step 2: Apply a light color of paint to each shutter with a foam brush. Allow to dry.

Step 3: With a second paint color, paint each shutter in a random pattern. This layering of coats creates textural interest and gives the shutters a weathered look. Allow to dry.

Step 4: Using a brush, lightly paint shutters with the top coat, allowing the other two hues to show through. Once dry, spray with polyurethane to seal. This technique instantly adds years to the appearance of the shutters. Allow to dry completely before hanging.

Lowe's
Shopping List

Materials:
- wooden shutters
- primer
- paint (in three colors of your choice)
- foam paintbrush
- paintbrush
- sandpaper
- polyurethane

PLANT LIFE

IF A GARDEN'S STRUCTURES provide its bones, plants flesh it out. With endless variations, plants add color, texture, movement, and fragrance. Placed correctly, they can focus views or dazzle with an eye-catching show. They cool down summer days and buffer frigid winds, affording us both comfort and shelter. Some plants attract wildlife, while others supply cut flowers and foliage that bring the garden indoors.

The best-laid gardens are not simply a group of individual plants, chosen for their unique properties, but a woven tapestry of color, form, and texture. Each plant adds a vital thread.

As you create your garden, remember that it will never be static. Unlike building materials, plants are ever changing. They bloom, change color, grow, and mature. Helping—and watching—this happen is the greatest reward of a well-designed garden.

plant categories

If you want a display that's more or less permanent, varying little from season to season, you'll want to choose shrubs, vines, small trees, and perennial plants; these are plants that can enhance a landscape all year—year after year—and respond well to pruning, shaping, and dividing.

For instant color to dress up your patio or to provide bright flowers and fragrance, you'll want to choose annuals. These flowering plants live only for a single growing season, providing a fresh start and look every few months.

Or you may want a combination of these approaches. You might select perennial plants and shrubs to provide a backdrop of interesting texture, foliage, and flowers, and then pair them with a changing assortment of annuals and bulbs for additional color.

Creating colorful container arrangements from the various plant categories—from annuals to trees to herbs—is discussed and illustrated on pages 104-108.

Annuals:
Masters of Seasonal Color

Sunny yellow marigolds, scarlet zinnias, and frilly pink petunias—when you think of color for your beds and containers, you naturally think of annuals.

Annuals are plants that complete their life cycle in one growing season. Because they're short-lived plants that you can buy at reasonable prices or even start from seed, you can feel free to experiment with them—to try various kinds and combinations. If you don't like the results, replacing them isn't too daunting. There are lots of ways to play with annuals. Try any or all of the following.

• Buy annuals in bloom to obtain almost instant color for a patio party or other special event or just for a spring or summer lift. Replace any spent plants with new ones that are coming into bloom.

• Use annuals to experiment with color. Try a combination of hot, bright colors or a soft pastel medley. Come up with some surprising pairings—such as red and purple annual salvia with pink and magenta verbena. Or try using only foliage color, mixing coleus with dusty miller and maybe purple-leafed 'Dark Opal' basil.

• Use annuals as blooming fillers in a bed with perennials; they'll provide plenty of color while the permanent plants are filling out or after they've finished their bloom season.

Perennials: Durable Mainstay

These are plants that grow and flower year after year. They are the mainstay of long-lived flowering borders and are surprisingly versatile, performing well in containers and among shrubs.

• Perennials have the advantage of carrying over from one year to the next. And they provide a sequence of unfolding foliage all yearlong.

• A perennial in a bed or border with annuals can take center stage when in full bloom, then recede to a supporting position as a foliage filler when the annuals bloom.

• Perennials are the obvious choice when predictability is a must, such as in foundation plantings and massed beds.

CLOCKWISE FROM TOP, LEFT: helianthus; chrysanthemums and marigolds; Siberian iris, bearded iris, chives, Shasta daisies, pansies, and petunias; dwarf narcissus and pansies; sedum; nandina; ornamental grasses, chrysanthemums, and marigolds

CLOCKWISE FROM ABOVE, LEFT: The larger the border, the less lawn to mow. A line of terra-cotta pots reins in this border. You can establish your border with native plants and materials. Perk up an empty spot with a pot of cheery annuals.

border magic

Mixing and matching colors of annuals and perennials is like painting with plants. If you have in mind a season-long pageant of riotous color, here are some useful strategies you may employ.

Use Shades of a Single Color

When you stick with one basic color, everything automatically goes together. Take purple, for instance. You can mix lavender, violet, and mauve flowers and plum-colored foliage splendidly—or pastel, rose, and cerise pinks. You can add accent colors later if you decide the look is too sedate. Here are some more suggestions.

• A pink-flowered spiraea with 'Apple Blossom' penstemon and pink coral bells (*Heuchera sanguinea*)
• Yellow iris and 'Coronation Gold' yarrow with yellow and cream columbine
• Burnished orange lion's tail (*Leonotis leonurus*) with bronze rudbeckia and a brown sedge, such as *Carex buchananii*
• Dark pink azaleas with pink Lenten rose and pink primroses

Use Complementary Colors

Colors that line up directly opposite from each other on the color wheel—red and green, orange and blue, yellow and violet—are always complementary pairs. Muting one or both colors makes the combina-

BIG LOOKS, *simple ideas*

FINIAL HOSE GUIDE

Start with a simple deck finial to create these easy hose guides for your borders. Remove existing screw from the bottom of the finial. Replace with a threaded steel rod of the appropriate size by screwing rod into the finial bottom. Spray-paint the finial in the desired color, and place in your border where desired.

WHAT A GREAT IDEA

SEVEN STEPS TO A BETTER BORDER

1. Make a plan. Determine the size of your bed or border, then sketch out a plan on paper. Mix together annuals, bulbs, perennials, and shrubs, arranging them according to height (low edgers in front, tall plants in the rear). Choose spiky-leafed plants for accents amid horizontal drifts and rounded clumps of annuals and perennials. Avoid a hodgepodge look by planting at least three of each plant. For a succession of blossoms, use spring-, summer-, and fall-blooming varieties.

2. Prepare the soil. A successful border begins with healthy soil. First, test the soil's drainage: Dig a 12-inch-deep hole, and fill it with water. If the water doesn't drain away in 12 to 24 hours, install a tile drain, plant in a raised bed, or choose a new site. Using a shovel or rotary tiller, turn the soil to a depth of about 12 inches. Mix in 2 to 4 inches of organic matter such as garden compost or well-composted manure.

3. Shop. Take your plan to the nursery. Choose small plants (six-pack-size annuals, six-pack or 4-inch perennials, and 1-gallon shrubs); they're more cost effective, and they get established faster than larger plants.

4. Arrange. Set the pots of perennials and shrubs out on the prepared soil. Make minor adjustments, and rearrange plants if some colors or textures don't work well together.

5. Set plants in the ground. Remove plants from the nursery containers. Loosen their root balls with your fingers, or, if the roots are circling, make several scores down the sides of each root ball with a knife. Dig holes, and place the plants in the ground, setting the top of the root balls even with the top of the soil. Fill in the holes; firm the soil.

6. Plant annuals and bulbs. Interplant bulbs among the perennials and shrubs. Overplant with cool-season annuals, so when spring comes, the bulb flowers bloom through them.

7. Mulch. Cover soil with a 2-inch layer of mulch to conserve moisture and help control weeds.

---

tions subtler. Apricot and lavender are easier to live with than orange and purple, for example. Following are some possibilities.
- Blue catmint with golden yarrow and buttery yellow Jerusalem sage
- Apricot foxglove and diascia with blue salvia and iris
- Reddish-blue leaves of *Loropetalum* 'Plum Delight' with chartreuse 'Sunset Gold' diosma *(Coleonema)*
- Bright gold Japanese forest grass *(Hakonechola macra* 'Aureola') with 'Blue Panda' corydalis and a chartreuse hosta and blue hosta

Use Color Echoes

This is the Mother Nature-makes-no-mistake approach. Choose a focal plant, and then build on its colors.

- Variegated 'Norah Leigh' phlox: Echo the foliage with cream-colored foxglove and the pink in the flowers with 'Evelyn' penstemon. Back the vignette with cream-colored roses.
- *Aster frikartii:* Back the lavender-blue of the flowers with the mauve haze of purple muhly grass, then pick up the asters' yellow centers with golden coreopsis.

Exclamation Points

If you plot out the shrubs and perennials you're considering on a piece of paper or in your head, you'll see that they all occupy oval or circular spaces. Add interest to your garden design by using the empty spots among the curving shapes to tuck in some vertical

plants—flowers that bloom along tall, leafless stalks.

Biennial foxglove, with its cluster of tubular flowers at eye level, is an example, and many iris fit into this category. These plants may put on only a brief performance, but they make up for it in showmanship. Consider the following.

- Lavender foxglove with pink roses and lamb's ears
- Pale blue delphiniums with dark blue salvia and *Iris pallida*
- Pale yellow *Verbascum bombyciferum* 'Arctic Summer' with yellow and pink alstroemeria and a true pink geranium such as 'Ballerina'
- Rose-pink *Watsonia* with pink rockrose *(Cistus incanus)* and *Artemisia*

Raised or terraced beds are relatively easy to create and can effectively disguise awkward slopes and dips in your garden. Raising the bed also gives you a quick way to establish a good soil foundation, because you must add soil to create the bed.

raised beds

Raising the garden above the ground can solve some of a gardener's most frustrating problems. Because you fill the beds with good soil to begin with, you're spared the labor and time of trying to improve hard or heavy soil. You can customize drip irrigation and soil amendments for each bed, depending on what you want to grow. You can protect plants from hungry critters by installing wire mesh beneath the bed or netting above. By elevating plantings along play areas, driveways, and paths, you also protect them from being kicked or run over. Raised beds add beauty, height, and interest to a flat landscape, and the variation from ground to bed level makes small gardens appear larger. And if stooping and kneeling are not high on your list of favorite gardening activities, you can design your beds with a wide cap on which to sit and work in comfort.

Size and Shape
Raised beds can be almost any size, but if you build them more than 4 feet wide, you'll have trouble reaching the middle from either side. For beds that will double as benches, a good height is 18 inches. Taller beds make good accents, but keep in mind that the higher the bed, the more expensive it will be to construct and fill.

Build freestanding beds any length, within reason; several smaller beds offer more design flexibility than a single large one. Beds that run along the length of a wall or fence can be as long as you like; the bed can even vary in height and width. To put gardening chores within easy reach of a wheelchair,

beds should be about 16 inches high and never wider than 4 feet. They can be rectangular or U-shaped, with the opening in the U just wide enough for a wheelchair.

Building Beds
You can locate a raised bed just about anywhere it will receive enough sun for the plants you wish to grow. This means about six hours per day for most warm-season vegetables (such as tomatoes) and other sun-worshippers. If you'll be hand-watering, don't stray too far from a water source, as soil in raised beds dries out faster than the same soil does in the ground.

It's easiest and quickest to make raised beds from wood—you can knock together a simple bed in less than an hour. Use rot-resistant woods such as redwood, cedar, or cypress (see pages 44-45) that is rated for ground contact. Brick beds are harder to construct—and you must build a concrete footing for them to rest on—but if your landscape features brick pathways, patios, or edgings, this can be a way to unify your garden design.

Another option is to construct a sturdy low bed with 2 x 6 lumber, and then use bricks around the outside of the bed, inserted in the soil at an angle, as an edging material. Beds made of flat stones or pieces of broken concrete suit informal gardens; if you keep the height low, you won't need to mortar the pieces together.

Commercial modular masonry systems, available in various styles and weights, are convenient for small, freestanding raised beds and entryways, especially because they can be easily formed into curves. Most use cast lips or interlocking pins that fit pieces together like a puzzle to hold the wall in place.

ABOVE: This raised bed creates a transition from the porch to the walkway below. Flagstones blend with their surroundings, harmonizing the extension of space.

Raised Bed Tips
To maximize the amount of sun plants receive, orient rectangular beds with their long sides running north and south.

For wooden beds, use 2-inch-thick (or thicker) lumber. Because the corners of the frame are the weak links, either lag screw them together or beef them up with pieces of 4 x 4s nailed to the inside of the corners. Beds more than 12 feet long need support to keep them from bowing outward, so nail the side boards to posts sunk midway along their lengths. If you're building multiple beds, make paths between them at least 2 feet wide.

If your garden soil is fairly good, fill raised beds with a mix of equal parts of soil and organic matter such as compost. Don't bother using poor soil; planting mix and topsoil are the best options.

Before filling the bed, place 3 to 4 inches of the new soil in the bottom, and mix it into the ground as best you can. This will aid drainage and create a transition zone between the two soils.

Whether casual and free growing or formal and manicured, a hedge can work just as well as a fence or wall to define areas, restrict movement, and provide privacy and protection from the wind.

green screens

Screens of hedges (upright growing shrubs) and vines define garden boundaries and are easier and less expensive to make than fences or walls. They contribute a lush look to a small space; they can be clipped into pleasing shapes or left to grow loose and wild. They change with the seasons, producing a flush of spring flowers or a topping of brilliant green new growth.

Before deciding on fast-growing plants, consider the extra maintenance they require. Vigorous, hardy hedges grown in a formal or semiformal style need almost constant clipping. Large, fast-growing hedg-

ing plants, such as Leyland cypress (*Cupressocyparis leylandii*), can quickly get away from you in a small garden. Instead, choose plants with more moderate growth rate, and fill in the gaps around them for the first two years with tall, quick-growing annuals and perennials, such as foxglove or cosmos.

Evergreen shrubs are the standard choice for hedges. They make plain backdrops for the decorative elements of the garden, and if you use the same plants for most of your screening, they will unify the garden and give it great structure. Where privacy is not a particular concern during winter, you might plant a deciduous hedge with fine flowers or fall foliage as a garden accent, or

perhaps plant a double hedge, with the decorative one backed by a taller, fine-textured evergreen one.

Formal and Semiformal Hedges

A formal hedge presents itself as a single unit with a smooth, sheared top and sides. You can clip it so that it's boxy, rounded, or pointed; in cold climates where snow load can distort the shape of hedges, a round or pointed top will help shed the snow. Because their growth is so restricted, formal hedges usually take up less space than semiformal or informal ones.

The best plants for formal hedging are rugged, small-leafed types, such as boxwood (*Buxus* sp.), yew (*Taxus*), hemlock (*Tsuga*), and

Most climbing plants can be easily trained to cover fences, arbors, walls, and trellises. Take care to choose a vine with a maintenance schedule that you are willing to meet. Many vines require serious pruning to keep them in check.

cate screens, whereas others know no bounds. A few monster vines, such as ivy, will cover a college building if left unchecked and may push up the roof shingles and work their way inside. It's not necessarily a bad idea to choose a fast- and rampant-growing vine, but it will need regular, heavy pruning in a small space.

Types of Vines

Vines are usually categorized by their climbing method. Some vines twine around supports naturally; they grasp on with tendrils, suction disks, or aerial rootlets. Others will need tying.

Twining vines twist and spiral as they grow, coiling around a slender support, themselves, or nearby plants. Most twining vines can't encircle a large post without some help. Honeysuckle *(Lonicera)*, jasmine, silver lace vine *(Polygonum aubertii)*, and Carolina jessamine *(Gelsemium sempervirens)* are all twining vines.

Clinging vines adhere tightly to surfaces by means of suction disks at the ends of the tendrils or by aerial rootlets along the stems. Boston ivy *(Parthenocissus tricuspidata)* and trumpet vine *(Distictis)* have suction disks at the end of tendrils; English ivy *(Hedera helix)* and climbing hydrangea have rootlets. Be careful where you plant clinging vines. They can get underneath and lift wood siding and weaken mortar joints between bricks and concrete blocks.

Vines with no means of attaching themselves, such as bougainvillea, will sprawl along the ground unless tied to a vertical support. Any kind of support will do, even a smooth wall if you can attach hardware to it to anchor the ties. Lead-headed masonry nails will even allow you to attach such vines to brick walls.

arborvitae *(Platycladus* and *Thuja)*, which are grown for their foliage rather than flowers or fruit. Their neat, finely textured appearance makes these evergreens a handsome backdrop to foreground plantings of flowers. Light and shadows play across their surfaces beautifully.

A semiformal hedge appears as a single unit, too, but the overall effect is softer, looser, and more billowy. This style is especially suitable for large-leafed plants, such as English laurel *(Prunus laurocerasus)*, which would get chopped and disfigured by close clipping for a formal hedge. Plants chosen for their flowers or fruit, such as myrtle *(Myrtus communis)* or holly *(Ilex)*, will provide a better show in a semi-

formal hedge than in a formal one, because you can prune to preserve some of the flowerbuds.

For an informal hedge, let the shrubs assume their natural shape, treating them just like individual plants that happen to be growing in a row. The informal style is the best choice for plants such as roses and cotoneaster that produce showy flowers or fruit, because you aren't constantly cutting off the flowerbuds. It's also the best choice for shrubs with an attractive growth habit, such as forsythia.

Choosing a Vine

Vines take up less ground space than hedges and can grow taller. Some vines are ideal for small, deli-

trees

Choosing Trees

Whether they are palms rustling near California beaches or sugar maples coloring New England mountain slopes, trees help define the general character of a landscape. They serve so many purposes—both aesthetic and practical—that few homeowners would consider doing without them. Trees offer cooling shade, provide shelter, and establish perspective. They can frame special vistas and block out unattractive ones. Trees can make dramatic statements, enhance the landscape with sculptural effects, and be the dominant feature of a landscape.

Although trees are often the most expensive individual plants to buy, they can be relied on to give permanence to any landscape. Not surprisingly, they are particularly valued in new housing developments.

Often overlooked is the role trees play in a house's energy conservation. For example, a tree-shaded house will require less air conditioning in summer than an exposed one. And if deciduous trees, which lose their leaves in winter, are planted around the south side of a house, the warmth of winter sunshine will be able to penetrate the interior of the house, helping to reduce heating and lighting costs.

Your choice of trees will be determined largely by the role you want them to play in your landscape. To block the sun, for example, select only trees that develop widely spreading branches. If you need a screen, look for trees that produce branches on their lower trunks, or combine shrubs or walls with trees that have bare lower trunks. For a focal point, choose a tree that displays flowers or fruits or one with

ABOVE: This sprawling flowering cherry not only provides ample shade all summer, but it delights with a brilliant canopy of color in the spring. RIGHT: A small crepe myrtle tucked into a corner can add a splash of fall color to an otherwise spent landscape.

attractive foliage, bark, or a striking winter silhouette.

Trees usually live for decades, even centuries. Each year, new growth springs from a framework of last year's branches to form a gradually enlarging structure. Tree silhouettes vary greatly from one species to another, and a tree's ultimate shape is usually not obvious in young nursery specimens.

Although the range of shapes is

enormous, all trees are classified as either deciduous or evergreen. Most deciduous types produce new leaves in spring and retain them throughout the summer. In the fall, leaf color may change from green to warm autumnal tones, and the trees then drop their foliage for the winter, revealing bare limbs. Broad-leaved evergreens, such as many magnolias, have wide leaves similar to some deciduous trees, but these cover the plant year-round. (Older leaves do drop however.) Evergreens include trees with needle-like foliage—firs, spruces, and pines, for example—and those with leaves that are actually tiny scales, such as cypresses and junipers. Because they keep their foliage in winter, evergreens retain their appearance throughout the year, although their colors may change slightly during cold months.

Planting

Select a healthy tree that will fit well into your landscape. Dig a hole wider than, but as deep as, the tree's root ball. Amend the excavated soil you'll use as backfill to create a transition between the soil in the container and your garden soil. Water, let drain, and then place the root ball into the hole. Fill in around the root ball with soil, and water thoroughly again. If necessary, stake the tree to keep it from tilting or falling over. Remove the stakes in about six months. Keep the soil moist around the roots until the tree is firmly rooted.

LEFT: Consider a tree's year-round range of color and form. While some trees, such as Japanese maple (above, left), display beautiful color in the fall, many evergreens vary widely in their hues and provide a yard with texture all year long.

PLANT YOUR TREE

After marking a wide circle, dig a hole to a depth equal to the height of the root ball. Amend the soil to be used for backfill, and score the sides of the root ball to loosen. Place the tree in the hole; fill with soil. A raised mound of soil around the tree holds water longer, allowing it to soak in.

ENJOY OUTDOOR LIVING

An area's personality doesn't come from plants and structures alone. Much depends on the addition of finishing touches, such as an antique olive jar, an old millstone, or a collection of handmade birdhouses. Accessories can range from formal and elegant, such as a Victorian bench or finely sculpted fountain, to a fun and folksy bottle tree or flock of plastic pink flamingos.

Garden ornaments have never been as plentiful or varied as they are today. You can find outdoor containers, furniture, lighting fixtures, and art at your local Lowe's store. Even a salvage yard can offer a treasure trove of accessories, with items such as old wrought iron gates, rusted metal sconces, cobblestones, sundials, and sculptures.

Create an outdoor retreat with the addition of seating, tables, and potted plants. An ornament or two will provide a touch of whimsy.

Add a grill and lighting for outdoor entertaining so family and friends can enjoy the ambience too. And don't forget a spot for the birds. Their colors and songs always delight visitors.

So set your imagination free. Let it run wild, in fact. Have fun choosing furnishings for your outdoor world. It doesn't have to be a jungle out there.

FURNISHING THE SPACE

OUTDOOR FURNITURE

There's an enduring graciousness to outdoor furniture. It evokes images of rolling lawns, intimate gardens, and lemonade in the afternoon. But deciding which furniture to buy can be a challenge.

Many styles are available in a range of materials that includes teak, woven willow, aluminum, wicker, and cast iron. Rustic furniture blends well with natural surroundings. Other styles are more finely crafted to complement patios and decks. Still other outdoor "furniture" comes not from a showroom, but from a gardener's imagination: Well-placed boulders, stones, and wooden planks also provide seating.

Consider the purpose your seating area will serve before selecting and arranging furniture. A hammock provides a place to ponder, while a picnic table is perfect for entertaining friends. No matter what your needs, there is a type of outdoor furniture to accommodate you.

Outdoor lounges, chairs, and tables often are designed in sets, with pieces priced individually. The price range can vary widely. Quality wooden furniture is sometimes more expensive than its cast-resin or metal counterparts.

Whichever you choose, keep in mind that it must be low maintenance because year-round exposure to sun, rain, insects, fungus, and smog account for heavy wear and tear.

If you want to sit and read or eat outside, you'll need patio chairs, tables, and benches. Patio-style wood furniture can be elegant and sturdy; it's also relatively easy to make yourself, if you're so inclined. You also can purchase wooden furniture, of course, along with resin and other types. Just make sure you take the climate into consideration—whether you are buying or building—durability is important in an outdoor setting.

When you just feel like whiling away those warm summer days in peace and serenity, find a shaded spot to hang a hammock—nothing beats it for old-fashioned comfort and style.

PLANNING SPACE

As you plan, allow sufficient space not only for the furniture, but also for the people using it. For instance, a person in a dining chair needs about 32 inches from the table to sit and rise comfortably. Two people sitting across from each other with a typical coffee table between them need about 8 feet.

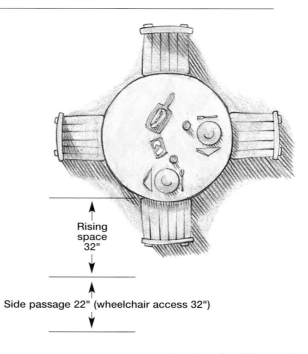

clearance around seats

Rising
space
32"

Side passage 22" (wheelchair access 32")

ABOVE AND BELOW: Sturdy outdoor furniture comes in a variety of materials, including aluminum and oak. BELOW, RIGHT: Even willow branches can be crafted into a place to rest after a long day.

CHOOSING THE RIGHT TYPE

One good way to narrow the daunting field of available outdoor furniture is first to consider the location and style of your area. For a patio off the house, coordinate the material to the style of the indoor furniture, and choose something as well crafted. For a rustic part of the garden, select country materials, such as wood or willow, or forget conventional furniture and use logs and flat-topped boulders.

Metal furniture used to mean Victorian-looking cast-iron benches that were cold and uncomfortable and too heavy to move. Nowadays, you can buy wrought iron furniture with metal mesh seats that have more give. Steel or cast-aluminum furniture looks heavy but actually is lightweight. Or look for enameled or powder-coated aluminum-frame furniture, which is lightweight and won't rust. Metal furniture can be found in either contemporary or traditional styles.

Wood furniture is natural looking and ages gracefully. Cedar and redwood are good choices because of their beauty, strength, and resistance to insects and rot, but to avoid depleting natural supplies, purchase only plantation-grown cedar or recycled redwood. Wood that needs paint or stain to preserve it can be colored to match the house or garden, but it's best to avoid white, because it causes too much glare in strong sunlight.

Furniture made of wicker or rattan is comfortable due to its natural flexibility, but the real thing is not durable enough to last outside a covered porch. Synthetic wicker, however, is impervious to weather, and it looks great.

Canvas director's chairs and deck chairs are really useful for a small space. They are more comfortable than folding French bistro furniture, plus they're portable, fairly tough, easily stored, inexpensive, and available in a wide range of fabric colors.

Be sure to check the chairs for comfort before you purchase them; some garden furniture is not sufficiently comfortable for leisurely outdoor living. Also determine how much maintenance the furniture needs; how durable it is in wet winters and whether it must be covered or stored indoors; whether the chairs and tables fold or stack; how easy the furniture is to move; how much space it occupies (do the chairs slide under the table when not in use?); and whether it is suitable for your sitting area floor (chairs with small feet may get stuck in the joints between paving units).

Protecting Wood Furniture

Water and sunlight are your furniture's worst enemies. Penetrating oils, varnishes, and paints are the finishes most often chosen to prevent water damage. Paint offers the most protection from the sun. Generally, the higher the gloss, the greater the sun protection. Some varnishes, such as spar varnish, contain UV filters that protect wood from the sun.

Furniture made of decay-resistant woods, such as redwood or cedar heartwood, may be left unfinished. They turn gray over time but require little maintenance other than scrubbing away dirt and mildew. Exposure can cause these woods to crack, however. To protect them and prevent graying and mildew, use a clear water repellent with UV protectors and a mildewcide. If you prefer the natural gray color, use a product with no UV protectors.

If you decide on a less decay-resistant wood, finishing will help to protect and beautify it. This will

WOOD FURNITURE DETAILS

Pay attention to the joinery when shopping for wood furniture. A sturdy joint (where an arm or chair leg meets the seat, for example) looks nearly seamless. And it is strong. It gives a chair, bench, or table the strength needed to withstand weight and side-to-side movement.

These photos show two types of quality joinery on wood furniture. Mortise-and-tenon construction secured with metal bolts and fasteners (top photo) ensures that the furniture is durable and of high quality. Metal cross supports (bottom photo) are key elements for the stability and support of table legs.

also keep insects from eating your furniture, and a colored topcoat conceals mismatched grain. Teak requires only periodic cleaning. Use a solution of dish soap with a small amount of bleach to clean away dirt. Maintain or restore like-new color with a sealer product made specifically for teak.

These roomy swivel chairs make it easy to shift attention from one person to a group of friends or to check on the whereabouts of young children.

OUTDOOR FURNITURE TRENDS AND TIPS

In recent years, manufacturers of garden and patio furniture have introduced innovative products that take outdoor living to a new level. Below are some new features to look for, along with shopping considerations.

Increased comfort. New outdoor furniture has actually been designed with people in mind. Features include cushions with springs and softer fabric. Chair backs are ergonomically angled, and many chairs come with ottomans.

Maintenance. Before you buy, remember that larger cushions require extra storage space. Because many chairs have springs, you'll want to take care not to let them get wet, so use them in sheltered or semi-sheltered areas. To keep upholstery looking fresh, dust often with a soft brush.

More movement. Outdoor furniture is rocking, rolling, reclining, and gliding in new ways. Bar carts, great for serving outdoor meals or beverages, are back in fashion. New accordion tables grow as needed, folding outdoor screens provide privacy, and even the tree-bound hammock has been rethought, making its home on porches or portable stands.

With a design emphasis on portability, these furnishings are perfect for the homeowner looking for privacy and the flexibility to create "rooms" within a large area. Keep in mind, however, that accessories such as screens and carts require large amounts of storage space during winter.

Material mix. For many years, outdoor furniture was either wood, aluminum, or plastic. Now you'll find pieces that mix all three. Combinations make use of the best traits of each material: The durability of plastic and aluminum is often paired with the warm good looks of teak.

You might have one piece of furniture with two different maintenance needs. If you want teak to hold its like-new color, you need to treat it with a special oil or stain. Aluminum and plastic simply need to be hosed off.

Contemporary lines. Many new outdoor chairs and tables draw their design inspiration from modernism rather than Mom's picnic table. Lines are often sleek and curvaceous, not chunky.

Use modern pieces in a setting where contemporary lines look at home. This furniture can sometimes be lightweight. While this can be an advantage in moving furnishings around, it does make them vulnerable to wind. Consider placing them in a protected area.

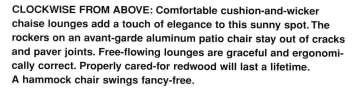

CLOCKWISE FROM ABOVE: Comfortable cushion-and-wicker chaise lounges add a touch of elegance to this sunny spot. The rockers on an avant-garde aluminum patio chair stay out of cracks and paver joints. Free-flowing lounges are graceful and ergonomically correct. Properly cared-for redwood will last a lifetime. A hammock chair swings fancy-free.

ABOVE: This outdoor lighting system guides visitors safely up the path to the entry. LEFT: The copper lanterns of this low-voltage system were easy to install. BELOW: The Oriental lantern is one of many styles available.

THE FACTS OF LIGHT

There's no need to leave your patio in the evening just because it's getting dark. Good lighting can extend your time outdoors for dining and play.

Outdoor lighting fixtures are either decorative or functional. Decorative lights—lanterns, hanging and post- or wall-mounted units, path lights, and strip lights—can add some fill light, but they're primarily meant to be seen, to set an architectural tone, and to highlight landscape elements.

A functional fixture's job is to light the setting without drawing attention to itself. It gives you the right kind of light for entertaining, outdoor cooking, or a lively evening volleyball game. Although some manufacturers make attractive versions, the less visible these fixtures are, the more successful your lighting will be.

Outdoor lighting also enhances safety. When it illuminates paths and steps, lighting decreases the possibility of missteps, and a well-lit yard is less attractive to intruders.

Lighting Basics

Although the principles are the same for both indoor and outdoor wiring, some materials used outdoors are specially designed to resist the weather. Drip-resistant subpanel boxes and waterproof switches, for example, remain safe in damp and wet locations, respectively.

Underground electrical cable has a thick solid-plastic covering that makes it watertight when buried directly in the ground. Typically, however, outdoor wiring is routed through rigid metallic and non-metallic conduit, protecting it from the weather and accidental damage.

You can bring electricity outdoors by extending a 120-volt power source from inside. Have your electrician tap into an existing switch, lighting fixture, or receptacle outlet box.

A simpler alternative is low-voltage lighting, operating on only 12 volts. The wiring is easy to install yourself and doesn't present the danger of 120 volts.

Whatever the system, use the protection of a ground fault interrupter (GFCI) on all outdoor circuits. Make sure you consult an electrician before you start work.

Standard Current Or Low Voltage?

Outdoor lighting can be powered by standard 120-volt current or by low-voltage systems with transformers that reduce household current to 12 volts.

Well suited for large projects or for lighting tall trees, standard-voltage fixtures often are better built and longer lasting than low-voltage models. However, they're also larger, harder to hide, more costly to install, more difficult to move, and harder to aim.

Any standard-voltage installation requires a building permit, and codes require that circuits be wired through GFCIs. Wires must be encased in rigid conduit unless they're at least 18 inches underground, and all junctions must be encased in approved outdoor boxes.

Advantages of low-voltage systems include energy conservation, greater safety, easier installation, portability, and more control of light beams. Some are solar powered.

On the down side, low-voltage fixtures often are simply staked into the ground and can be upset or fall over. The number of lamps that one transformer can power is limited by voltage drop over distance.

Outdoor lights come in many styles, colors, and finishes. All are made to hold up well when exposed to the elements.

Deciding Where You Need Light

Start by determining how much of your yard you want to light. Most lighting designers divide the garden into three zones: a foreground, which usually is given mid-level brightness; a middle ground, with low-level light and an interplay of shadows; and a background—often the brightest—to draw the eye through the garden.

Lighting should never be spotty. It should define, not disguise. For example, uplighting gives a tall tree a dramatic form, but it also can make the top appear to hover spectrally above the earth. To visually anchor the trunk, illuminate it near ground level.

Be aware of how your lights affect the neighbors. Some communities even have ordinances regulating "light trespass."

Following are suggestions for common lighting situations.

Walks and Steps. Softly lit walkways won't divert focus from nearby decorative lighting. Low fixtures that spread soft pools of light are effective. Incorporating them into plantings along the edge of the path can showcase features of your yard at night and camouflage the fixtures during the day. Steps also can be lit by these fixtures, or by ones built into the risers of the steps themselves or into a retaining wall alongside the steps.

Dining and Living Areas. Dim lighting is usually appropriate for quiet conversation or outdoor dining. Soft, indirect lighting provides enough visibility to see without robbing the evening of its mood. Cooking and other high-activity areas require brighter lighting.

Foliage. Uplighting, downlighting, and spread lighting are common techniques for illuminating foliage. Using separate switches and dimmers allows for a greater variation of effects.

For a dappled "moonlight" effect, place both uplights and downlights in a large tree to accent some of the foliage and to create shadows on the ground. To

The lights around this home serve a variety of purposes—spotlighting plants, adding a warm glow to a flowerbed, and lighting a walkway for safety. In addition, they provide security.

ABOVE: The lights of this patio shine on through trees and plants to create dramatic shadows. BELOW, LEFT: A hooded downlight is mounted on a branch to shine on plants below. BELOW, RIGHT: Lighting the outdoors can be as easy as running a string of lights along your deck railing.

silhouette a tree or shrub, aim a spotlight or wall washer at a fence or a wall behind the plant.

Try Mini-lights. Decorative mini-lights highlight trees and define other features while lending sparkle to the area.

Avoid Glare. The discomfort you feel when looking at a light that's too bright or that's aimed straight at your eyes is caused by glare. Use careful light placement and fixture selection to avoid this situation.

The best way to avoid glare is to place fixtures out of sight lines, either very low or very high—along a walk or up in a tree, for example. Direct the fixtures so that only the effect of the light is noticed, not the light itself. Try to avoid bright spots of light. They are less inviting and create more glare.

Use More Fixtures. Use a few strategically placed low-wattage lights outside the entryway rather than one high-wattage light.

Incorporate Shielded Fixtures. In a shielded fixture, the bulb is completely hidden by a shroud that directs light away from the viewer's eye. You see the warm glow of a lighted object rather than a concentrated hot spot of light.

Nuts and Bolts

The low-voltage transformer, usually housed in an integral drip-resistant box, steps down the household current of 120 volts to 12 volts. Plug it into a nearby receptacle, then run the 12-volt cable from the low-voltage side of the transformer to the desired locations for your lights. The cable can be buried a few inches deep in the ground or simply covered with mulch in a planting area; however, to avoid accidentally spading through it, consider running the cable alongside structures, walks, and fences where you won't be likely to cultivate.

A low-voltage system often comes in a kit with lights, cable, and transformer. Some light fixtures clip onto the wire. Others require a clamp connector, while still others must be spliced into the system and connected with wire nuts. Use the wire and connections specified in the instructions. If you don't already have a receptacle to plug the transformer into, install a GFCI-protected receptacle.

Sizing Your System

Most 12-volt transformers are rated for loads from 100 to 300 watts. The higher the rating, the more light fixtures you can connect to the transformer. In most cases, you add

ABOVE: Lanterns made to hang inside an open umbrella light up the tabletop rather than casting shadows from behind your guests.
BELOW: Portable candlelit torches and lanterns lend an exotic atmosphere and make it easy to create just the right mood.

up the wattage of all the light fixtures you wish to install, then choose a transformer and cable size that can handle the load.

For long cable runs, however, you must de-rate the circuit to account for "voltage drop"—the accumulated resistance in all that wire. A voltage drop up to 10% (1.2 volts) is considered acceptable—more than that, and you'll see noticeably less light output.

How can you combat voltage drop? For starters, you might try a larger wire size. Or plan to run two or more shorter cables in a "split-load" pattern. You also can install multiple transformers and/or circuits. It isn't necessary to place two transformers side-by-side. One

Specialty lights can direct traffic along an entryway or dress up an empty corner of your patio. You can purchase them, create them from decorative items you already have, or craft them from something as simple as a paper bag.

For example, a string of six 20-watt fixtures served by a 60-foot run of #12 cable would be calculated as follows: 120 (6 x 20 watts) x 60 (feet) divided by 7,500 (the cable constant of #12 wire) = .96 volt. This is less than the allowable voltage drop of 1.2 volts, so all is well. But a 150-watt load that runs 50 feet on #14 cable computes as: 150 x 50 divided by 3,500 = 2.14. This voltage drop is too high. Subtract a fixture or two, plan a shorter cable run, or increase wire size.

Portable Lighting

Special occasions sometimes call for temporary lighting that can be placed spontaneously and without regard for the electrical infrastructure. A wide range of lanterns is available, from oil-burning hurricane lamps to glass-sided lanterns that house candles. Thanks to improved photo-voltaics, movable footlights with batteries charged by the sun are now available.

Most people are familiar with classic Mexican luminarias—the open paper bags that contain votive candles set in sand. Now, however, safer electric luminarias are available, adding to the growing field of specialty outdoor lighting. Tiny lights on strings bring a carnival atmosphere to a patio or deck. Lanterns on stakes add drama along the path to a gate or door.

No matter which lantern you choose, you'll need to place it with care; this is especially true for lanterns with open flames. Avoid placing lanterns along a path or among foliage where they can pose a fire hazard. Make sure that they are sturdy and will not topple over in a breeze. And avoid putting metal lanterns that could become hot near dry plant material.

might be pole-mounted in a remote location that's fed by 120-volt cable or wires, allowing a much shorter low-voltage run.

Figuring Voltage Drop

Professional designers and electricians figure voltage drop in a number of ways. The easiest method is to multiply the wattage by the distance the cable will travel, and then divide that figure by the cable's so-called "cable constant," which takes the product's inherent resistance into account.

Cable constants for typical low-voltage gauges are as follows.

#16 wire	2,200
#14 wire	3,500
#12 wire	7,500
#10 wire	11,920

OUTDOOR KITCHENS

Dining outdoors seems to sharpen the appetite and add spice to even the simplest of meals. While the informal mood of an outdoor party eases the burden on the host, a formal dinner gains extra cachet when served beneath a garden marquee or under a starry sky.

If you're a dedicated outdoor chef with enough space—especially if you live in a climate that allows year-round outdoor cooking and entertaining—you might want to plan for a permanent outdoor kitchen.

In addition to built-in cooking facilities, amenities include preparation and serving counters, storage cabinets (for cooking mitts and various barbecue utensils), and perhaps a refrigerator and a sink.

A great advantage of these permanent installations over portable barbecues is that they usually operate on piped-in natural gas, rather than containers of propane or charcoal (either of which can run out at inconvenient moments).

Layout and Design

In colder or windier climates, an outdoor kitchen—like the nearby dining area—should have good protection from the elements. The site should take advantage of existing protection, such as the side of the house, a wall of the garage or potting shed, or the corner where a wing meets the main house. Fences or natural wind screens such as hedges can reduce the influence of prevailing winds and provide late-afternoon shade. In warm climates, open the area to breezes to help ensure comfort.

Remember that no matter how well-appointed your outdoor kitchen is, some of the food will be prepared inside and the leftovers

ABOVE: If you have the space and your climate is suitable much of the year, an outdoor kitchen will beckon you to dine in the open air with family and friends. RIGHT: Tile countertops withstand the elements and add a splash of color to this outdoor kitchen.

will be returned there later. With this in mind, outdoor cooking areas should be easily accessible to the indoor kitchen. Smooth, well-tended paths leading from the house are crucial for shuttling back and forth (a serving cart will also make this much more convenient). Use the base plan to place your kitchen, as well as dining and other outdoor living areas, in the best locations.

To help keep outdoor cooking facilities clean, choose materials carefully. Glazed ceramic tiles, for example, are an excellent choice for countertops. Wood, on the other hand, should be avoided. Materials used for counters, fireplaces, or fire pits should also complement house and patio building materials. For instance, if you plan to build your new area with bricks, they

should match the bricks used in nearby walls or paving.

The layout of your outdoor kitchen and your choice of cooking elements will depend on your favorite cooking technique, whether you prefer grilling, stir-frying, or griddle cooking. More sophisticated masonry units incorporate built-in smokers, commercial-quality woks, or pizza ovens that accompany the traditional grill. So-called ultimate grills feature latest technology components such as high-output side burners, smoke injectors, and infrared heating elements.

Facilities around the barbecue could include preparation and serving areas, storage cabinets, a vent hood, an under-the-counter refrigerator, a sink with a garbage disposal, a dishwasher, a wet bar, and a place

as concrete and tile so that you can clean the kitchen area simply by hosing it down. (Install watertight electrical outlets out of the way of routine cleanup.)

Most outdoor kitchens are at least partially sheltered by a simple overhead structure or housed in a gazebo. Depending on the site's exposure and microclimate, you may need to add screens, trellises, or even heavy-duty sliding doors to help block wind and hot sun or provide temporary enclosure during winter months.

Electricity and Plumbing

Install lighting much as you would for an indoor kitchen. Effective downlighting illuminates preparation areas; other fixtures, perhaps dimmer-controlled, can create the ambience desired for a dinner party. Decorative mini-lights add a background glow and provide safety when other lights are off.

You must route water-supply pipes, drainpipes, and electrical cable or conduit to the outdoor kitchen. In cold climates, pipes should be insulated or equipped with valves at low points to facilitate drainage in winter. Drainpipes must slope toward the main drain, which may be difficult, depending on the existing drainage layout. Electrical wiring must be shielded.

Outdoor electrical outlets, light fixtures, and switches must be protected by watertight boxes. In addition, all outdoor outlets must be protected by a ground fault circuit interrupter (GFCI), which shuts off power to the circuit in case of an electrical short.

If you're planning an extensive kitchen addition outside, it's best to consult a landscape architect or contractor familiar with such additions.

ABOVE: This outdoor kitchen and eating area offer the ultimate in alfresco dining experiences. LEFT: With an efficient design and suitably sized appliances, an area for outdoor food preparation can be tucked into almost any corner.

to eat. An L- or U-shaped layout allows for buffet counters and dining peninsulas with ample storage shelves and cupboards beneath. Built-in entertainment centers with TV or audio/intercom systems are other possible additions.

Maintaining and cleaning outdoor cooking facilities can be a challenge. Use protective grill covers and rugged building materials such

LEFT: This massive outdoor fireplace adds a touch of splendor to its natural surroundings. ABOVE AND RIGHT: Grills are available with multiple cooking surfaces that allow you to grill while keeping food warm and preparing dishes on other burners.

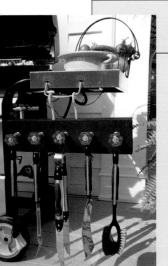

BIG LOOKS,
simple ideas

GRILL TOOL CADDY

Create a simple but creative organizer for keeping your grill tools handy.

Cut a 2 x 4 to the appropriate length to accommodate the number of tools you need, then paint the entire board with black exterior paint. (Our five tools needed a board approximately 22 inches in length.)

Use a Forstner ¾-inch drill bit at even increments down the center of the board to create holes for ½-inch boiler valves. After drilling the holes, dip the backs of the valves in a mixture of liquid dishwashing soap and water; push the valves through the holes. To hang the board from the grill handle, attach large yellow overhead-storage hooks.

OUTDOOR GRILLING

The center of most outdoor dining is the barbecue grill. Barbecuing exists in all cultures in some form, because it is just one step from cooking over a simple, open fire. Mediterranean cooking, for example, with its kabobs and seafood dishes, provides an exotic approach to backyard menus.

Even the standard fare of hamburgers is easily fancied up. A Texas-style barbecue is a genre unto itself, featuring hearty meals of chicken and ribs, prepared with western panache. The following pages present the techniques of grilling outdoors, with information on an amazing range of cooking possibilities.

Shop Smart: Grills

Do you want the perfect fire at the touch of a button? Or do you take great pride in your ability to get the flames started and keep them properly tended while you cook? Do you appreciate precise temperature adjustments, or do you savor that hands-on, do-it-yourself challenge?

When shopping for a grill, think of the tasks you will be doing, and consider the special features you would like to have. You can purchase different types, so narrowing your search is important. Here are some suggestions to guide you.

Quality

Choose a company with a good reputation. These manufacturers stand behind their products and generally have responsive customer service departments when you need accessories or replacement parts.

Charcoal

Cooking over charcoal creates a more intense smoked flavor, but it takes longer to reach the proper cooking temperature. It is hard to control the heat while cooking, and it requires substantial attention from the chef. Cooking this way also takes more time. After lighting, you should be able to cook in 15 to 30 minutes, depending on the size of the grill and the number and type of briquets. Quality grills have vents to control the cooking temperature. (**NOTE:** Charcoal briquets produce carbon monoxide. Never use these grills indoors.)

Gas

Gas grills are as easy to use as they are to clean and control. They offer all you could want in convenience and safety. Gas grills use a liquid propane tank or natural gas. This cooking system virtually eliminates

flare-ups and offers ultimate control of cooking temperatures. Although propane tanks do need to be refilled, in the long run using gas is less expensive than buying charcoal. Both propane and natural gas grills offer years of safe operation if properly maintained. It is important to check these grills for leaks. (**Note:** To check for leaks, make a water-and-liquid soap solution. Turn on the gas at the tank only, and brush the solution over the tank, hose, and all connections. If bubbles appear, there is a leak. The damaged part should be replaced immediately.)

Gas grills ignite quickly, usually with a push-button lighter integrated into the grill. After about 10 minutes of preheating, the grill is ready for cooking. A standard liquid propane tank should last about 15 hours when set on high temperatures. Gas is also less messy than charcoal, and there are no ashes to empty. Best of all, when you are finished cooking and turn off the grill, the heat dissipates quickly. You don't have to wait for the coals to cool to secure the area.

Where To Grill

No matter which grill you choose, it should be located outdoors, well away from any flammable materials. Avoid areas with a roof or with overhanging trees. Do not grill in the garage, carport, on a porch, or within 10 feet of the house.

Grill Safety

Always use caution when lighting a grill to prevent accidents. A gas grill gets very hot, about 800°F.

Place a layer of bricks or a concrete slab under a charcoal grill when placing it on a wooden deck. This will prevent hot embers from falling and setting fire to the deck.

The classic kettle charcoal grill can be found in a variety of sizes. Wheels make it easy to move around.

A Cadillac among grills, this stainless steel gas version has four burners, a thermometer, a warming basket, and concealed storage.

This grill offers a swing-up surface, four burners, a wire storage shelf, and wheels for easy mobility.

Its compact design makes this charcoal grill easy to pack up for camping or tailgating.

OUTDOOR DINING KNOW-HOW

Sure, you're competing with the bugs for your share of the food. In fact, when it comes to bugs you *are* the food. But even with an insect skirmish or two, outdoor dining can be a treat. Consider some of these tips for your next soiree.

Serving Suggestions

Ice-cold drinks are crucial for successful summer gatherings. Look through your garden shed for clever coolers: Park a wheelbarrow near the serving table, or place some elegant urns in suitable spots—both are perfect for icing down bottled or canned drinks. You also should consider them for keeping ice cream or watermelon slices cool for hours. If

ABOVE: A well-organized buffet makes it easy for your guests to help themselves and move quickly through the serving line. BELOW, LEFT: Hose off your wheelbarrow, and create a drink station that rolls. BELOW: This lemonade stand for the kids doubles as a refreshment cart when you're entertaining.

TURN TO PAGE 124 OF THE WORKBOOK TO LEARN HOW TO MAKE A CHILD'S MOBILE LEMONADE STAND.

ABOVE, LEFT: Put both your indoor and outdoor kitchens to use, and you'll have an impressive meal ready for guests in no time.
ABOVE, RIGHT: Turn an urn into a cooler for icing down drinks.
BELOW: Dine poolside even when the weather's too cool to take a dip.

you plan on serving beverages in glasses, simply fill one of these containers with ice, and let your guests help themselves with a clean new garden trowel.

If you're serving from a sturdy table or potting bench, line urns with aluminum foil or plastic wrap; then turn them into elegant containers for fruit salad or tortilla chips. And just because you're dining outdoors doesn't mean that the rules of buffet placement no longer apply. Set your serving table properly, and traffic will flow smoothly.

Place food on a round or oval table so that the guests will move in a circle as they serve themselves. You should begin the buffet with a stack of plates, followed by the meat or main dish (don't forget the serving utensils), then vegetables, salads, and other side dishes. Condiments and bread come next, followed by glasses, silverware, and napkins.

If you're using a long table, speed things up by setting up matching buffets on either side so two lines can serve at the same time.

BIG LOOKS, *simple ideas*

OUTDOOR LANTERNS

Draped in tissue paper, these lanterns can be tailored to any color scheme. If you're using a red tablecloth, choose a rosy paper. Blue hydrangeas on your table? Try shades of purple and blue.

What you'll need: white glue, water, scissors, tissue paper, glass jars, 16-gauge steel wire, wire cutters, and tea lights.

Mix 1 part glue to 2 parts water. Don't worry about getting the mixture exactly right—the process is forgiving.

Cut the tissue paper into rectangles, then dip each rectangle into the glue mixture.

Arrange the rectangles on the surface of the jars, letting the second rectangle overlap the first and so on, until the jars are covered. Let dry.

Wrap one piece of wire around the neck of each jar, and attach a U-shape second piece to make a handle. Place a tea light inside each lantern.

Potluck Picnic Savvy

When attending a potluck, choose dishes that can be made ahead or assembled at the last minute, preferably those that taste good at room temperature. Supplement with ready-to-serve items such as breads, crackers, cheeses, olives, pickled vegetables, fruit, and deli salads.

Keep a picnic basket or box packed with basic supplies: plates, cutlery, cups, napkins, tablecloth, bottled water or other beverages, salt, pepper, sugar, paper towels, moist wipes, and trash bags. Include temperature-retaining vessels and insulated bags for hot and cold items. Store gel packs in the freezer to keep foods cold; replace the packs in the freezer when you return. Food transported cold or hot can stand on the table up to two hours.

To serve 8, there should be an appetizer, a salad, an entrée, and a dessert. For 16, include two of each item. For 24, include three of each.

Dining Accessories

Once all else is in place—the dining and serving tables, the grill, shade or insect protection—you can focus on simple refinements that elevate the ordinary to the memorable. For example, use potted plants or festive tablecloths.

BIG LOOKS,
simple ideas

STARS-AND-STRIPES TABLECLOTH

Show your true colors with this all-American stars-and-stripes stenciled tablecloth. For a 3-foot-square table, cut a 6-foot square out of a 9- x 12-foot canvas drop cloth. With scissors, snip a fringe ¼-inch deep around all four edges of the cloth. Machine-wash the canvas in cold water, and dry it on medium heat (the canvas will shrink about 6 inches). The edges will be frayed unevenly, so you'll need to trim them with scissors until they are fairly uniform. From poster board, cut a star shape and stripe pattern in the desired size to make a stencil. Determine even spacing of your flag design along the edges of the cloth, and mark with a pencil to use as a guide when stenciling. Using permanent acrylic colors and a stencil brush, paint the design with a dabbing motion. Paint all the blue stripes first, let dry, and then paint the red stars.

BIG LOOKS,
simple ideas

HERBS IN LABELED POTS

Identify your plants and seedlings with this clever chalkboard-pot herb garden. Prepare four 4-inch terra-cotta pots and saucers by turning them upside down and spraying with primer. Allow them to dry, and then spray evenly with chalkboard paint. When dry, repeat with a second coat of chalkboard paint. Turn saucers right side up, and spray the inside with primer and two coats of chalkboard paint. For the wooden base, use a sponge brush to paint a ½- x 6- x 24-inch craft board cherry red. Let dry, and add a second coat. Paint the rims of the pots and saucers with the same red paint—these will require two to three coats. When the paint dries, plant with your favorite herbs or seedlings, and write their names in chalk directly on the pots. (You can even make note of special watering or feeding needs.) The chalkboard surface wipes clean easily with a damp cloth.

FINISHING TOUCHES

TODAY'S DESIGN-CONSCIOUS gardeners, when seeking to enhance their outdoor environs, are met with a myriad of choices. Everywhere are objects and features designed to beautify gardens and complement plantings. Fountains, carved stepping-stones, mosaic-encrusted urns, and gazing globes are just a few of the temptations. To that add pieces you already own, such as a statue, a weathered wood plaque, or peeling window frame discovered at a garage sale. But how do you combine these objects without producing a jumble?

Accessories lend a garden its character, so let your personality guide you in your selections. Choose only the objects that you really love. If you're crazy about a certain piece—whether it's a ceramic animal or a stately stone fountain—it will

Individual accessories, such as a gazing ball or whimsical metal-and-glass sculptures, infuse a garden with the owner's personality and style.

be right at home in your garden.

Still, it's a challenge to combine those personal choices with other elements, such as plants, furnishings, and the hardscape of walks and walls. Sometimes you plant to complement an ornament; other times you use a piece to harmonize with the plantings you have. Some features, such as fountains, gazebos and arbors, will be permanently sited; others, such as pots, birdhouses and some statuary, can be moved from spot to spot to keep the scheme of the garden fresh.

BIG LOOKS, *simple ideas*

LEAVES IN STONE

The path to your favorite spot in the garden is the perfect place to display stepping-stones imprinted with leaf designs. First, build a simple wooden form to fill with mortar. Then create designs by pressing leaves into the damp mortar.

Use leaves with interesting shapes and thick veins that will create good imprints. Hydrangea, sassafras, viburnum, sweet gum, maple, and oak leaves produce nice designs. Add a concrete dye or dabble a bit of wood stain on the leaf print to give it color and definition.

Step 1: For the sides of the form, use 2-inch-wide ¾-inch-thick pieces of wood. (You can have a 1 x 4 ripped to 2 inches in width at the lumberyard. The actual thickness of the wood will be approximately ¾ inch.) Cut four pieces of wood, each measuring 18¾ inches in length. Place the end of one piece at a right angle to another, drill a pilot hole, and insert a 1¼-inch-long screw. Add the other two pieces of wood to form a square. Cut one (18¾-inch-square) piece of hardboard. Drill pilot holes, and attach to the bottom of the frame.

Step 2: Add water to mortar mix, following manufacturer's instructions.

Step 3: Fill the wooden form with mortar. Select a scrap of wood that's a few inches longer than the form, and pull it across

the surface to smooth the mortar.

Step 4: Place a concrete joint tool, trowel, or screwdriver at an angle on the edges of the stepping-stone and draw it along to bevel them. This will keep the edges of the stone from chipping easily.

Step 5: Pick several fresh leaves in a variety of sizes, and press them into the surface of the mortar. Let the leaves remain until the mortar is firm but not completely set.

Step 6: Peel leaves from the mortar, and let it harden completely. Remove screws joining the hardboard to the form; unscrew one side, and take out the stone. Reassemble the form so it will be ready to use again. To darken the leaf shapes, simply apply diluted green or brown wood stain or earth-tone latex paint.

Lowe's Shopping List

- drill and drill bits
- concrete joint tool
- wood screws
- mortar mix
- assorted leaves
- wood stain
- 1 (8-foot-long) piece ¾- x 2-inch wood
- 1 (18¾-inch-square) piece hardboard

CLOCKWISE FROM ABOVE: Select garden art that appeals to you, and then find a special spot to display it. A vintage chair (to be used to hold a planter), stone spheres, droll statuary, and metal leaf sculptures are just a sampling of the many choices. You might not know what you want until you run across it.

GARDEN ART

Like icing on a cake, the right garden art can transform a seemingly ordinary garden into a magical hideaway. Whether it's a playful gargoyle standing guard over a pond or small rocks nestled on the ground among baby's tears, an outdoor sculpture can serve as a visual oasis. Even a topiary can turn a humble herb garden into a charming outdoor room. The key is to select pieces that fit your garden's style.

Look in outdoor-sculpture galleries for larger, more expensive pieces. Major metropolitan areas and small towns known to be artists' havens usually have at least one such gallery. Some artists also sell out of their studios. Specialty garden shops and interior design and gift stores also are excellent places to hunt.

For the budget minded, Lowe's offers a good selection of sundials; birdhouses; painted or sculpted wall plaques; and wood, metal, or stone statues. Wonderful bargains also can be found in salvage yards, antiques shops, and thrift stores.

Display Basics

The size and shape of the ornament or art piece help determine how best to set it off. Large sculptures can sit on the ground, stand on a pedestal or platform, or bask in the center of a fountain or pool.

If you collect a variety of objects, vary their positions and heights in the garden. A rock sculpture placed on the ground or a birdhouse hanging from a branch can add cheerful and surprising touches to otherwise overlooked areas.

Keep the backdrop simple. No matter where you put outdoor art, make sure the surroundings are simple enough to display it properly (hedges and solid-color walls work very well).

Check it out. After you buy a piece of art and take it home, try it in different locations to see where it looks best.

Keep scale in mind. A massive piece requires plenty of space around it to prevent it from dwarfing its neighbors, while a small ornament can easily get lost in a jungle of foliage.

ABOVE THE ORDINARY

Pots of trailing flowers and other small treasures often deserve a boost. But large platforms or ornate pedestals may steal the limelight from the objects they support. This homemade pedestal has simple lines that allow it to fit into almost any garden space.

Three 4-foot lengths of 5-inch-diameter wooden poles, cut from standard 8-foot poles, form the pedestal; they're connected by 10-inch-long 3/8-inch lag bolts that run through 3/4-inch copper pipe couplings.

Viewed from overhead, the pedestal's three poles form an equilateral triangle; together, the pole tops provide a surface wide enough to hold pots as large as 18 inches in diameter.

Whether your garden has its own natural water element or you have to create one, allow the water to extend and echo the existing area as these water features do. The formal reflecting pool at right was located in a small space to make a bold statement.

THE MAGIC OF WATER

Almost any garden can benefit from the addition of a water feature. Whether captured and directed through lively fountains and small streams or gathered into quiet ponds, water brings coolness and serenity to its surroundings. It's no wonder that water was a prominent element in the ancient gardens of Rome and Persia, as well as in the later gardens and landscapes of Europe and Asia. Cascades, pools, and fountains were principal features in Renaissance Italian gardens, just as pools and canals were central to the great gardens of France and England. In Chinese and Japanese gardens, microcosmic bodies of water imitated the natural world by representing oceans, lakes, and rivers on a small scale.

While water has inherent beauty and appeal, structures such as fountains and pools used to contain and direct it also add charm. For example, a pool and fountain made of colorful tiles is highly decorative. The sight of sunlight playing on the falling water adds another dimension

The difference in tone of the water features above and below might be vast, but both successfully reflect the feel of their respective surroundings.

of pleasure. You may design a formal garden around such a fountain, or you may choose a water feature that looks as if nature left it there by happy accident. Even a small basin with a simple spout trickling water brings joy.

You can devise a water feature for any garden. Whether a tub of water containing a few aquatic plants or a cascade tumbling over native rocks, water elements are as versatile as they are effective. Visit Lowe's Garden Center to learn more about these products.

WHAT A GREAT IDEA

PORTABLE TRANQUILITY
Waterfall Container Garden

Bubbling water brings a peaceful atmosphere to any space, indoors or out. This small, self-contained water feature starts with a shallow planter. Add rocks, a waterfall, and some tropical plants to make your own soothing fountain.

Step 1: Spray a 14-inch plastic planter bowl with a stone-colored spray paint. Allow planter to dry thoroughly, then apply a second coat and allow to dry.

Step 2: Cover the bottom of the planter with a thin layer of rocks. Next, add potting soil, filling planter about half full. Level the soil with your hands, and place the slate waterfall at one edge of the planter. Remove or add soil until the edges of the planter and waterfall are even.

Step 3: Select several companion plants suitable for the light conditions where the waterfall garden will be located. Starting with the larger or trailing foliage, insert around the outside edge of the waterfall bowl. Add smaller plants to fill in the bare areas.

Lowe's Shopping List

- 14-inch-diameter plastic planter bowl
- stone-finish spray paint
- river rocks
- slate waterfall
- creeping fig
- spray bottle
- potting soil
- bromeliads
- sheet moss

Step 4: Place sheet moss over any exposed soil. With scissors, cut moss to fit, allowing extra to hang over the edges of the planter. Hide electrical cord from waterfall under the moss, and let the cord hang from the backside of the planter. To secure moss, add river rock to bare areas and around the base of plants.

Step 5: Mist plants with water to remove loose soil, and then place container garden in the desired location. (Once water has been added, the container becomes too heavy and awkward to lift.) Add water to the fountain until bowl is half full. Dry hands completely, and test water flow by plugging in the pump. Adjust the pump to raise or lower the height of the water. The higher the flow, the louder the sound of the fountain.

Step 6: Once the waterfall is running, move moss away from water flow; otherwise it will soak up large quantities of water.

Different types of birdhouses appeal to different types of birds. Unless your birdhouse will be purely decorative, spend some time researching the birds you want to attract before building it. Or, if you're feeling serendipitous, just build the style that appeals to you most, and see what it attracts.

BIG LOOKS, *simple ideas*

BIRD FEEDERS

Use eye-catching feeders to welcome birds. Fill three cedar bird feeders with two different varieties of birdseed, alternating between a wild birdseed mix and sunflower birdseed. Hang the feeders at staggered heights.

BIRDHOUSES

Like weather vanes and sundials, birdhouses can be as much art as accessory. They come in many styles, from wooden antiques to late-model metal. Whimsical houses are fun to look at but might not work as living spaces for birds.

Only cavity-nesting birds (those that nest in tree hollows) use birdhouses. This group includes bluebirds, chickadees, nuthatches, swallows, and wrens.

The kind of house you install determines the kinds of birds you'll attract, but this is an inexact science. While a birdhouse may be intended for a wren or a bluebird, it will be fair game for any bird of similar size.

Small birds, such as chickadees, nuthatches, and most wrens, prefer a hole that is 1⅛ inches across. Medium-size birds, such as bluebirds

and swallows, need a nest box with a hole of 1½ inches. White-breasted nuthatches need 1¼ inches; mountain bluebirds need 1⁹⁄₁₆ inches.

Tree swallows and violet-green swallows accept a wider variety of habitats, often stealing houses from bluebirds. Larger birds, such as purple martins and flickers, take boxes with 2¼- and 2½-inch entry holes, respectively. Flickers usually like to dig out their own nests, but sometimes you can attract them with a large nest box. Fill it with wood chips; they'll dig it out.

Birdhouse Basics

To keep birdhouses safe from raccoons, cats, and other predators, mount them atop metal poles. If you want to put a birdhouse in a tree, hang it from a branch.

Keep birdhouses away from feeders (the mealtime bustle makes nesting birds nervous).

Face the entrance away from prevailing weather, and remove any perch your birdhouse came with. (It's unnecessary, and house sparrows use it to heckle birds inside.)

Birdhouses should be made from materials that insulate well, such as 1-inch-thick wood. (Plastic milk bottles and milk cartons are too thin and have poor ventilation; heat can bake chicks inside or make them fledge too early.)

Nest boxes need a side or top that opens for easy cleaning, drain holes on the bottom, and vent holes

high in the sides for hot weather.

If you put up more than one, keep houses well separated and out of sight of one another.

Houses must go up early, because migrant birds start returning in late February and look for nest sites soon after they arrive.

MOSAIC BIRDHOUSE

Choose a birdhouse with a simple design. Select about eight edging tiles in two or three colors of your choice. Place the tiles in a heavy-duty zip-top plastic bag, and break into small pieces with a hammer. Glue the pieces to the front of the birdhouse with Liquid Nails, and let dry overnight. Fill the gaps between the tiles with white tile grout. After 15 minutes, wipe the surface clean with a damp sponge. Paint the rest of the birdhouse in the paint color of your choice. Sand lightly for an aged look. Remove the chain and bottom piece from a decorative pull chain (in the lighting section). Attach it to the top of the birdhouse with Liquid Nails (removing a finial, if necessary).

Container gardening makes it easy to change your plants with the seasons or to move them around, adding color to empty corners. Place a large pot where you want it, and then plant. Or place your already-filled pots in a cart and move them as needed.

WHAT A GREAT IDEA

FIVE STEPS TO GREAT POTS

1. Select a color scheme. Choose colors to suit a holiday or event. Or take your design cues from the surroundings: paving, walls, furnishings.

2. Determine the location. Combine large and small pots in clusters around patios, on steps, and by doorways. Use odd numbers—groups of three and five pots—for striking vignettes. Make sure that the scale of the containers is in keeping with the site.

3. Buy quality planters. Try glazed containers or Italian terra-cotta. Secondhand and antiques stores are good sources for unusual containers.

4. Plant the pots. Fill the pots partway with a good potting mix. Mix in a controlled-release fertilizer, and then plant. Think of each pot as having a grid dividing it into three sections—back, center, and front. Plant the tallest plant in back, two medium-size plants in the center on either side of the tallest plant, and a cascading plant in front. Tuck intensely colored annuals and bulbs on either side of the cascaders. Use potting mix to fill in around plants.

5. Water after planting. Keep the soil moist. Once the plants fill in, small pots might need watering daily. If you start with young plants, feed them with 0-10-10 fertilizer (following label directions) after two weeks.

GARDENING IN POTS

Container plants make the kind of garden that anyone can grow. If you're a beginner, container gardens are the perfect way to take the plunge. You can start small, and then move on to more ambitious projects at your own pace. For the experienced gardener, containers offer the joy of unlimited possibilities for experimentation.

Potted plants allow you to have a garden when space is limited. Even gardeners with plenty of room value the versatility they offer. Blooming pots bring seasonal color to garden beds, a porch, or the front steps. Plants too tender for winter can be moved to shelter when cold weather hits.

Displaying Big Containers

When they're bursting with blooms, large containers can command as much attention as flowerbeds. But to show them off to best advantage, you need to put them in the right

Plants in pots or flower boxes work well either individually or in groups of several. You can dress up a railing or a stoop with a few well-placed pots, or you might mass containers together to give the impression of a flowerbed planted around a pathway or along steps.

BIG LOOKS, *simple ideas*

PAINTED WATERING CAN

Turn plain watering cans into colorful works of art with paint or rub-on transfers. Before painting your watering can, wipe it with mineral spirits, and then spray with primer. Tape with painter's tape to create an even border around the top and bottom of the can. Carefully apply two coats of craft paint, making sure to remove the tape before the paint is completely dry. For the polka-dot pattern, use different sizes of round foam stencil brushes. (Tip: After painting the nozzle, insert toothpicks into the holes to keep them from being blocked.) With a sponge brush, apply an even coat of polycrylic over the entire can to seal.

You can use rub-on transfers to achieve a different effect. First, remove the nozzle from the can, and spray with primer before spraying with two coats of craft paint. When the paint dries, cut out a strip of transfer border (wrap it around the base of the watering can to measure for length). Follow the manufacturer's instructions to apply. Cut out individual shapes from a sheet of transfers, and press them onto the can to create your pattern. Apply, following the manufacturer's instructions. Reattach the nozzle, and apply an even coat of polycrylic over the transfers and painted area to seal.

spot. Placement against a plain background—such as paving, walls, lawns, or foliage—enhances their colors and shapes.

Big plant-filled pots are useful in many situations. They can adorn structures, add interest in front of a hedge, break up open spaces, or serve as portable color to hide a work in progress. They can direct traffic and serve as barriers and focal points.

These portable gardens are perfect solutions for paved-over areas where plants otherwise won't grow, such as beside a front door, along an expanse of paving, or where pavement meets a house or garage wall.

Two containers can make a welcoming display on either side of a front walk, an entry, or a doorway. A single large container planting offers a handsome focal point in the corner of a deck or patio or at the end of a still pond, where its image is reflected in the water.

Nestle a big pot among flowering perennials in a border, and you can fill out a temporary bare spot or add height to low plantings.

Lightweight containers from Lowe's make it easier to move large arrangements.

Container Gardens for Shade

Not every container garden has to bask in brilliant sunlight in order to shine. If your deck, porch, or patio is shaded, you can create container combinations every bit as colorful as their sun-drenched counterparts—as evidenced by the arrangements shown here.

When you shop for shade plants at Lowe's, head first for the sheltered display area—that's where shade-loving plants will be featured. Then take a look at the houseplant section. Plants in full or partial shade don't need watering as often as pots in full sun, so you may get away with watering them every two or three days instead of daily.

sunshine in shade

PROVING THAT even shade-loving plants can add warm, sunny color to the garden or patio, big blooms of yellow and red tuberous begonias glow amid lush green foliage plants. Red flowering maple and impatiens blossoms add more spots of color. The interplay of leaf textures brings an extra dimension of interest to this well-designed pot. In cold-winter areas, overwinter the pot indoors, or treat it as you would annuals, and start over with new plants in the spring.

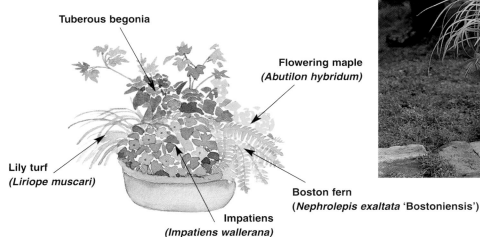

Tuberous begonia

Flowering maple
(Abutilon hybridum)

Lily turf
(Liriope muscari)

Boston fern
(Nephrolepis exaltata 'Bostoniensis'*)*

Impatiens
(Impatiens wallerana)

leafy symphony

FOLIAGE PROVIDES ALL THE COLOR AND FORM necessary for this knockout composition of color and pattern. The bold green leaves of hosta make a dramatic statement; the variegated foliage of houttuynia and ivy, in colors both brilliant and subtle, enliven the composition, while the coleus chimes in with its own deep red notes.

Pinch and trim the coleus, ivy, and houttuynia as needed to keep the plants balanced. Although all these plants are technically perennials, the coleus is generally treated as an annual; replace it with a new plant when it fades.

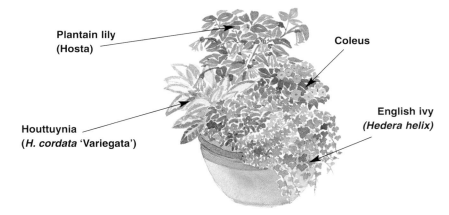

Plantain lily
(Hosta)

Coleus

English ivy
(Hedera helix)

Houttuynia
(H. cordata 'Variegata'*)*

double-decker herb pot

HERBS ARE A COOK'S BEST FRIENDS and a gardener's delight. You'll get double-duty from a pot filled with texture and color to please the eye, as well as scents and flavors to pique the palate.

This two-tier planting, overflowing with herbs, was created by stacking one bowl-shaped terra-cotta container atop another. The pots used here are 16 and 24 inches across; whatever sizes you use, be sure the bottom pot is large enough to allow plenty of planting room. Plant taller herbs in the top pot, and add cascading and low, bushy plants in the bottom tier.

The arrangement shown below concentrates on basil, one of the easiest herbs to grow. Basil thrives in warm and hot weather, producing an abundance of attractive foliage over a long season. Special Italian varieties; dwarf basil from Greece; and basils with lemon, licorice, or clove scents are interesting varieties to try.

For a fast start, buy herbs in 2- or 4-inch pots. Many kinds, including basil, can also be grown from seed. Pinch back the growing tips of basil plants for bushiness, fertilize regularly, and pinch off flowers.

classic bouquet

SPILLING OVER WITH BLOOMS, this bouquet-in-a-pot is a charming mosaic of small-scale flowers in rainbow hues; the myriad points of color seem to sparkle in the sun. The texture of the plantings is light, airy, and delicate. Clouds of flowers float above and outside the boundaries of the simple terra-cotta pot, while small-leafed ground ivy trails over the pot's edge, carrying out the scale and mood.

This one-season arrangement will grow lush and full in the bright summer sun. The key to keeping it looking its best is regular deadheading and shaping throughout the growing period. With a little attention, the blooms will be abundant and dense and the plant shapes full yet controlled.

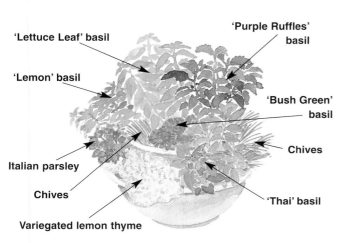

'Lettuce Leaf' basil
'Purple Ruffles' basil
'Lemon' basil
'Bush Green' basil
Chives
Italian parsley
Chives
'Thai' basil
Variegated lemon thyme

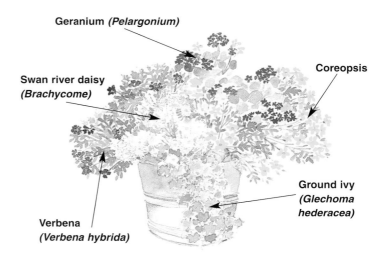

Geranium (Pelargonium)
Coreopsis
Swan river daisy (Brachycome)
Ground ivy (Glechoma hederacea)
Verbena (Verbena hybrida)

fruits and flowers

A SMALL TREE can be the centerpiece of a dramatic large-scale container design. This one features a handsome 'Nagami' kumquat—known in China as a good-luck plant. The kumquat is an excellent, versatile container specimen. It bears loads of sweet, showy fruit, and in spring, it's covered with richly perfumed white blossoms. The dense foliage is attractive too. Here the shrubby plant has been pruned and trained to display a rounded shape atop a single trunk.

The centerpiece tree is underplanted with blooming plants that spill over the container's edges, adding splashes of bold color and giving balance to the design so that it doesn't appear top-heavy.

A planter for a small tree should be at least 18 inches across; this square concrete container is a generous 22 inches.

Because the kumquat is fairly tender (to about 18°F), be prepared to move the entire container indoors if you live in a cold-winter area. (In fact, this is one kind of citrus you can grow indoors year-round, given bright light and sufficiently moist air.) If your climate allows you to keep this arrangement outdoors all year, the flowering plants can be left in the container. But they are short-lived perennials, often treated as annuals, and will need replacing after a couple of seasons.

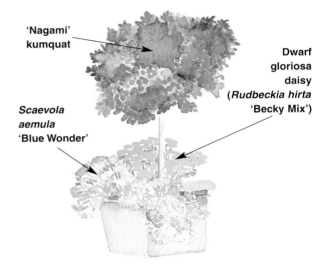

'Nagami' kumquat

Dwarf gloriosa daisy (*Rudbeckia hirta* 'Becky Mix')

Scaevola aemula 'Blue Wonder'

BIG LOOKS,
simple ideas

GARDEN STAKES

Give your plants a boost with these handsome garden stakes constructed from copper tubes adorned with drapery finials. Start by encircling one end of a ½- x 24-inch copper tube with duct tape. Tear the tape so that it measures about ¾ inch wide, and wrap so that the tape rises slightly above the lip of the tube. Continue wrapping until the tape creates a tight fit for the finial of your choice. Remove the screw from the finial's base, and use it to press the tape over the tube's edge and into the center, creating a relatively flat surface on top. (You may discard the screw, or save it for another use.) Dab the taped surface of the tube with Liquid Nails, and press the finial firmly on top. Now the stake is ready to take its place in your garden.

WORKBOOK
IDEAS YOU
CAN BUILD

We know you've been inspired by the numerous projects and ideas offered within the pages of this book. Regardless of your skill level, landscaping challenges, or lifestyle, we're sure you've found ideas you want to incorporate into your outdoor living space. That being the case, we're happy to supply complete instructions for several of the featured projects. Each has step-by-step directions and a handy shopping list to simplify your trip to Lowe's. Helpful illustrations and cutting lists for lumber are included where necessary. We know you will enjoy the fruits of your labor.

Note: Use caution when constructing these projects and other projects that may require treated lumber. See page 45 for guidelines.

mobile sandbox

as featured on page 53

Your children will enjoy hours of imaginative fun with this mobile sandbox. Casters allow you to slide the sandbox into the shade, move it into the garage during winter, or pass it along when your children have outgrown it.

The lid creates a play surface and keeps sand free of debris; metal pulls make it easy to remove. Locking casters both mobilize and stabilize.

Step 1: Legs & Skirt Construction

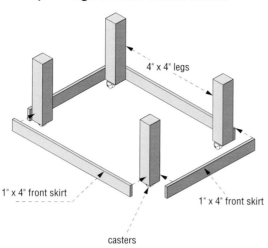

4" x 4" legs

1" x 4" front skirt

1" x 4" front skirt

casters

WOODWORKING TIP

When drilling pilot holes for screws, and especially lag screws, size the drill bit to the body of the lag screw instead of the width of the threads. This can be easily done by holding the bit in front of the screw and looking at both of them together. If you can see threads on both sides of the drill bit, it will be the proper size.

Do not overtighten the screw. Once this happens, the wood is stripped and the screw will not hold. If this should happen, a trick used by carpenters is to remove the screw and insert a wooden match in the hole, breaking the match off flush with the top of the hole. The screw can then be reinserted, using the new wood as filler.

Width of threads

Size of body

Proper size bit for this screw

Step 2: Bottom Shelf Construction

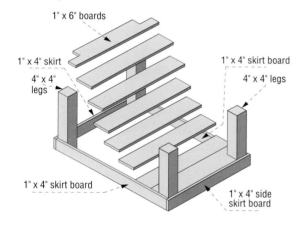

1" x 6" boards

1" x 4" skirt

4" x 4" legs

1" x 4" skirt board

1" x 4" skirt board

1" x 4" side skirt board

4" x 4" legs

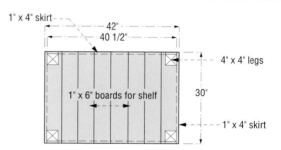

1" x 4" skirt

42"

40 1/2"

4" x 4" legs

1" x 6" boards for shelf

30"

1" x 4" skirt

Top View Bottom Shelf

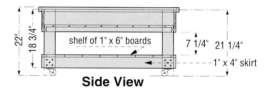

22"

18 3/4"

shelf of 1" x 6" boards

7 1/4"   21 1/4"

1" x 4" skirt

Side View

Instructions

Step 1: Assemble skirt and legs (see cut list, page 112).

a. Use wood glue to attach the bottom front skirt board flush with the bottom ends of two legs. Reinforce using 1¼-inch screws.

b. Repeat Step 1a to attach the bottom back skirt board to the other two legs in the same manner.

c. Glue the two bottom side skirts flush with the ends of the front and back legs and skirts. Reinforce with 1¼-inch screws.

d. Attach casters to bottom center of each leg by centering casters on leg bottom and marking the four holes. Predrill, then attach with lag screws. (See "Woodworking Tip" above.)

Step 2: Build bottom shelf. Measure and mark the top center of the front and back skirt boards. Center the first

bottom shelf board on this mark. Attach with wood glue and 1¼-inch screws. Attach the rest of the bottom shelf boards, working outward from the center board. Trim last boards to fit around each leg.

Step 3: Construct sandbox portion.

a. Attach 40½-inch-long front and back sides at the tops of the legs using wood glue and 1¼-inch screws. All top edges should be flush.

b. Repeat Step 3a to attach the 30-inch-long sides at the tops of the legs in the same manner.

c. Cut to fit, and attach twelve 1- x 2-inch cleats to the inside bottom of the front, back, and sides, and to the inside of the legs at the same level using 1¼-inch screws and wood glue.

d. Attach 1- x 6-inch tongue-and-groove boards to cleats using 1¼-inch screws and glue. Center first board as in

Step 3: Sandbox Portion

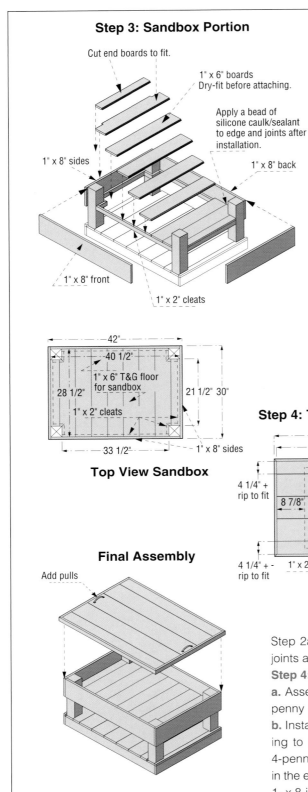

Cut end boards to fit.

1" x 6" boards
Dry-fit before attaching.

Apply a bead of silicone caulk/sealant to edge and joints after installation.

1" x 8" sides

1" x 8" back

1" x 8" front

1" x 2" cleats

Top View Sandbox

- 42"
- 40 1/2"
- 1" x 6" T&G floor for sandbox
- 28 1/2"
- 1" x 2" cleats
- 21 1/2"
- 30"
- 33 1/2"
- 1" x 8" sides

Final Assembly

Add pulls

CUT LIST*

Part	Material	Size	Quantity	Notes
legs	mailbox posts	18¾ inches	4	with casters
bottom skirt	1 x 4	40½ inches	2	front and back
bottom skirt	1 x 4	30 inches	2	sides
bottom shelf	1 x 6	30 inches	8	
sides	1 x 8	40½ inches	2	front and back
sides	1 x 8	30 inches	2	sides
cleats	1 x 2	cut to fit	12	
bottom	1 x 6	28½ inches	8	tongue-and-groove
edge band	1 x 2	44 inches** approximately	2	miter (front and back)
edge band	1 x 2	32 inches** approximately	2	miter (sides)
top boards	1 x 8	42½ inches	5	
cross braces	1 x 4	26 inches	3	

*Measurements from nominal lumber sizes.   **Cut to fit.

Step 4: Top Cover Construction

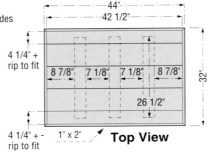

- 44"
- 42 1/2"
- 4 1/4" + rip to fit
- 8 7/8"
- 7 1/8"
- 7 1/8"
- 8 7/8"
- 32"
- 26 1/2"
- 4 1/4" + - rip to fit
- 1" x 2"

Top View

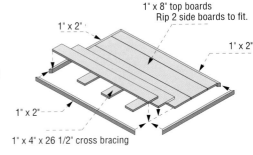

1" x 8" top boards
Rip 2 side boards to fit.

1" x 2"

1" x 2"

1" x 2"

1" x 4" x 26 1/2" cross bracing

Build edge frame first ensuring corners are square.

Step 2a. Note: Cut end boards to fit, and dry-fit before attaching. Seal joints and edges of sandbox using silicone caulk/sealant.

Step 4: Construct top cover.

a. Assemble 1- x 2-inch edge band frame (miter corners) using 4- or 6-penny galvanized finishing nails and glue; check for square.

b. Install 1- x 8-inch top boards starting with the center board and working to each edge. The edge boards will have to be ripped to fit. Use 4-penny galvanized nails. (**Tip:** Cut and lay dry the 1- x 8-inch top boards in the edge band frame, then attach the 1- x 4-inch cross braces. Nail the 1- x 8-inch top boards to the edge band.)

c. Install 1- x 4-inch cross braces with 8⅞-inch spacing using 1¼-inch galvanized screws and glue. (**Note:** Center cross braces, leaving approximately a 2-inch gap on each end.)

d. Add pulls centered on top cover.

decorative doghouse

as featured on page 52

Your pet will feel right at home in this delightful doghouse. We added classic details, but it's easy to customize this traditional design to fit your pet's style.

Your family pet will be the envy of the neighborhood with his custom-made home. Building this doghouse can be a project involving the whole family.

Getting Started

Cut all pieces according to the cut list (page 116) and the illustrations.

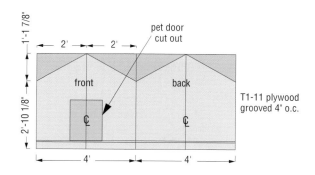

1'-1 7/8"
2'
2'
pet door cut out
front
back
C
C
2'-10 1/8"
4'
4'
T1-11 plywood grooved 4" o.c.

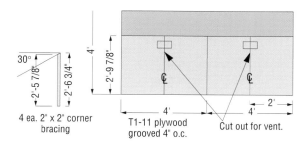

30°
2'-5 7/8"
2'-6 3/4"
4'
2'-9 7/8"
2'
4'
4'
C
C
4 ea. 2" x 2" corner bracing
T1-11 plywood grooved 4" o.c.
Cut out for vent.

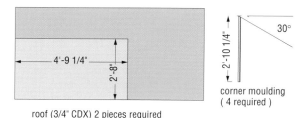

4'-9 1/4"
2'-8"
roof (3/4" CDX) 2 pieces required

30°
2'-10 1/4"
corner moulding (4 required)

Frame Assembly

[see illustration 1]

Building a raised platform allows the structure to sit enough above the ground to prevent water from entering. If the ground is not level, use stakes as supports in order to make the doghouse level. You may want to try placing the house on cinder blocks as another support option.

Step 1: Nail the four 2 x 4s together to assemble the frame. (**Note:** The side pieces will overlap the ends of the front and back pieces.) Check for square.

Step 2: Align the top of each support flush with the top and against the inside edges of the 4-foot-long front and back pieces of the platform, and nail them together. (See diagram below.)

Step 3: For the floor, cut ¾-inch-thick plywood to fit over the frame, making sure it is flush with the edges. To complete the base, attach the plywood to the top of the frame using 1¼-inch screws every 6 inches.

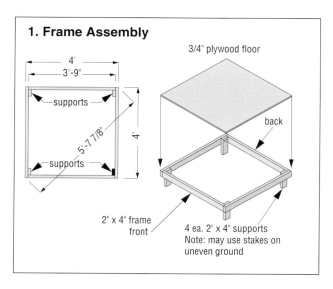

1. Frame Assembly

4'
3'-9"
supports
5'-7 7/8"
supports
4'
3/4" plywood floor
back
2" x 4" frame front
4 ea. 2" x 4" supports
Note: may use stakes on uneven ground

Lumber
- 2 (10-foot) 2 x 4 boards
- 1 (8-foot) 2 x 4 spruce board
- 3 ($^{23}/_{32}$-inch-thick) 4- x 8-foot BC pine CDX exterior plywood
- 2 ($^{19}/_{32}$-inch-thick) 4- x 8-foot pine siding (T1-11 grooved at 4 inches o.c.)
- 3 (8-foot) 2 x 2 spruce boards
- 1 (8-foot) 1 x 2 spruce board (for filler)

Millwork
- 2 (8-foot) 1- x 1-inch prefinished outside corner moulding
- 2 (8-foot) $^5/_8$- x 1$^5/_8$-inch shingle moulding
- 1 (8-foot) $^3/_8$- x $^3/_4$-inch dentil edge moulding*
- 2 ($^1/_2$- x 2$^1/_2$-inch) Victorian corner blocks
- 1 (8-foot) $^3/_8$- x 2$^1/_4$-inch fluted casing*
- 1 embossed wood carving

Paint
- Severe Weather Exterior Primer
- house paint (American Tradition, Montpelier Ashlar Gray, exterior, semigloss)
- trim paint (American Tradition, Montpelier Madison White, exterior, high gloss)

Miscellaneous
- super-large pet door
- 2 (4-x 8-inch) closable air conditioning vents
- solar-powered hanging garden accent light
- 2 (5- x 3$^1/_2$-inch) black shelf brackets
- flower pot

Roofing
- 2 packages (20-year, 3-tab) asphalt roofing shingles (Slate)
- 1 roll (15-pound) asphalt roof felt

Fasteners
- 2 (1-pound) boxes $^7/_8$-inch galvanized roofing nails
- 1 (1-pound) box 1$^1/_4$-inch exterior wood screws
- 1 (1-pound) box 4-penny galvanized finishing nails
- $^1/_2$-inch zinc wood screws
- 1 (1-pound) box 6-penny ring-shank exterior box nails

Tools
• tape measure	• pencil	• sandpaper
• straightedge	• circular saw	• clamp
• jigsaw	• hammer	• drop cloth
• drill	• miter box	• paintbrush
• shingle utility knife	• drill bits	

Similar moulding profile available in most stores.

2. Sides & Corner Bracing Assembly

side

corner brace

back

Attach brace with screws.

front

side

Attach sides to base with 4-penny finishing nails.

Sides & Corner Bracing Assembly

[see illustration 2]

Step 1: Using the diagrams provided, draw dimensions for front, back, and sides onto the sheets of grooved plywood. Carefully cut out the panels.

Step 2: Following the manufacturer's instructions, cut out an opening for the pet door on the front panel of the doghouse. Make sure bottom of opening is at least 3$^1/_2$ inches up from bottom of front panel. (**Note:** Do not install the pet door at this time.)

Step 3: Cut out holes for closable vents, centered and 4 inches down from top of each side.

Step 4: Attach front and back panels to frame with 6-penny ring-shank exterior box nails, making sure edges are flush and bottom edge is flush with bottom edge of frame assembly.

Step 5: Attach the 2- x 2-inch corner braces flush against the short end of the front and back panels, making sure the mitered edge is at the top, facing toward the side pieces. Secure braces to front and back panels using 1$^1/_4$-inch screws every few inches. (**Tip:** Clamps will help here.)

Step 6: Align one side piece with front and back of platform. To attach sides, nail bottom into frame, then screw into the 2- x 2-inch braces in the corners using 1$^1/_4$-inch screws every few inches.

Classic architectural details, such as this fluted molding and corner rosettes, create a grand doggy entrance.

3. Ridge, Top Bracing, & Roof

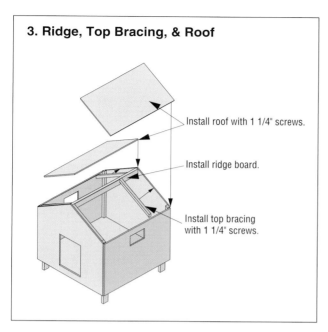

Install roof with 1 1/4" screws.

Install ridge board.

Install top bracing with 1 1/4" screws.

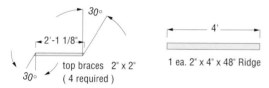

30°
2'-1 1/8"
30°
top braces 2" x 2"
(4 required)

4'
1 ea. 2" x 4" x 48" Ridge

Ridge, Top Bracing, & Roof
[see illustration 3]

Step 1: You now have a doghouse with no roof. Check the inside to make sure there are no exposed nails or screws.
Step 2: Place the ridge in the middle to run across and support the top edges of the plywood roof pieces, making sure it doesn't extend above the roof line. Attach using 1¼-inch screws.
Step 3: Using 1¼-inch screws, attach top braces. These will be used to connect the plywood roof to the rest of the structure.
Step 4: Attach the left panel of the roof. Secure it in place with 1¼-inch wood screws into the top bracing. Attach the right roof panel. Check front and back overhang for equal spacing before attaching.

Corner Moulding, Vents, & Pet Door
[see illustration 4]

Step 1: Using 4-penny galvanized finishing nails in predrilled holes, attach corner moulding to cover the exposed corners.
Step 2: Install air vents in each side of the house, using ½-inch zinc wood screws. Make sure louvers point down when open.

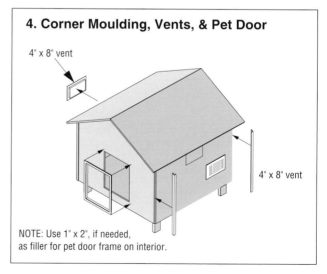

Decorative details can make your doghouse a lovely fixture for the yard. To this one we added a light and a carving over the door. Vents cool in the summer.

4. Corner Moulding, Vents, & Pet Door

4" x 8" vent

4" x 8" vent

NOTE: Use 1" x 2", if needed, as filler for pet door frame on interior.

Step 3: Attach the pet door following manufacturer's instructions, making sure not to leave any exposed screws on the inside. (Add filler as needed to the opening of the pet door frame if front panel is not thick enough.) Use ½-inch zinc wood screws, if necessary.

Final Trim, Roofing, & Brackets

Step 1: Attach shelf brackets using ½-inch screws. Hang a solar-powered light on one bracket and a metal bucket with flowers on the other.

Step 2: Add shingle moulding under the eaves of the house, fluted casing and corner blocks around the door, and dentil moulding along the front and back edges of the roof, using 4-penny galvanized finishing nails in predrilled holes.

Step 3: Paint the doghouse before adding shingles, and allow to dry.

Step 4: Tack roofing felt over entire roof, then install shingles. Slate-colored (20-year, 3-tab) asphalt shingles were used for the doghouse shown here because they absorb less heat than darker ones. When installing shingles, always start from the bottom and work up. Run the first row of shingles along the bottom edge of the roof upside down to show a finished edge at the bottom. Place the next row directly on top of the first row. Cap the ridge with cut shingle tabs to prevent leaking. (**Note:** Use short roofing nails, making sure they don't protrude on the inside of the doghouse.)

Step 5: Check entire inside of doghouse for protruding nails or screws.

CUT LIST

Part	Material	Size	Quantity	Notes
supports	2 x 4	8 feet	4	#2 SYP
frame front/back	2 x 4	4 feet	2	#2 SYP
frame sides	2 x 4	3 feet 9 inches	2	#2 SYP
floor	(¾-inch-thick) 4- x 8-foot plywood panel	4-foot square	1	CDX plywood
front	(19⁄32-inch-thick) 4- x 8-foot pine siding	see illustration	1	T1-11 grooved 4 inches o.c.
back	(19⁄32-inch-thick) 4- x 8-foot pine siding	see illustration	1	T1-11 grooved 4 inches o.c.
sides	(19⁄32-inch-thick) 4- x 8-foot pine siding	4 feet x 2 feet 9⅞ inches	2	T1-11 grooved 4 inches o.c.
corner brace	2 x 2	2 feet 6¾ inches	4	miter 30-degree angle at one end; spruce
ridge	2 x 4	48 inches	1	spruce
top brace	2 x 2	2 feet 1⅛ inches	4	miter 30-degree angle off ends; spruce
roof decking	(¾-inch-thick) 4- x 8-foot plywood panel	4 feet 9¼ inches x 2 feet 8 inches	2	CDX plywood
corners	corner moulding	2 feet 10¼ inches	4	miter 30-degree angle at one end
moulding	dentil edge	miter to fit	4	optional
moulding	shingle	miter to fit	4	optional
moulding	fluted casing	cut to fit around door	3	optional

fence and arbor

as featured on page 59

These plans will give you a well-built arbor gateway and coordinating fence. They can be easily adapted for various heights and landscape situations.

Arbor Gateway

Step 1: Determine the size you want. The one pictured here is 10 feet 6 inches high with a 5-foot-wide opening.

Step 2: Measure and mark the centers of the two gateway posts. Add the width of one post to the desired gateway opening to get posthole center marks (5 feet 5½ inches in this case).

Step 3: Dig a 12-inch-diameter hole about 36 inches deep for each post, centered on marks.

Step 4: Place several inches of small gravel (8-9-10) in the bottom of each hole, and tamp.

Step 5: Set one post in hole, and plumb using a post level or 2-foot level. Use a diagonal brace attached to the post and a stake in the ground to hold the post plumb in each direction. Repeat with other post.

Step 6: Measure the height of each post to make sure there is enough post above ground for desired height.

Step 7: Mix and pour concrete around each post, tamping lightly to remove air bubbles. Crown the top of the

Give your family and guests a grand entrance to your yard with this elegant arbor and matching fence.

concrete around each post to divert moisture from post (see illustration). Let concrete set before continuing.

Step 8: Measure for desired post height (in this case, 107 inches from the ground). Take the overall desired height and subtract 19 inches from this to get post height (126 inches - 19 inches=107 inches). Posts do not go to the peak of the roof.

Step 9: Cut one post off at the desired height. Use a straight board and level or a string level to transfer this height to the other post. Mark and cut other post.

Step 10: To construct a top band box for the roof frame support, fasten a mitered 24- x 4- x 6-inch post flush with

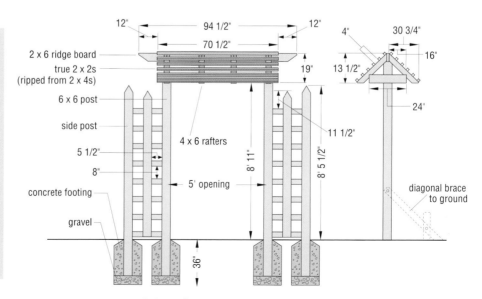

Arbor Gateway Elevation

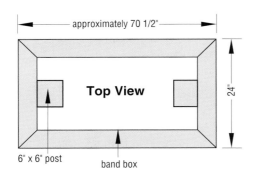

approximately 70 1/2"

Top View

24"

6" x 6" post

band box

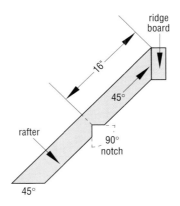

ridge board

16"

45°

rafter

90° notch

45°

the top of each post, centered on the post and level (put the 6-inch side flat to the post).

Step 11: Measure from the long end of each mitered 24-inch piece, and cut a long, mitered 4- x 6-inch board to connect to each and complete the top band box. Fasten at each corner with exterior glue and 16-penny galvanized finishing nails.

Step 12: The roof frame consists of a 2- x 6- x 93-inch ridge board and eight 4- x 6- x 30¾-inch rafters. Using scrap 2 x 4s, make a temporary brace centered on each end of the top band for the 2 x 6 ridge board, with its top 13½ inches above the top of the top band centered on each end. Place the 2 x 6 ridge board on top of these braces, centered on the gate opening. Temporarily fasten in place with screws.

Step 13: Centering an end rafter over each gateway post, fasten to the ridge board and the top band using 16-penny galvanized finishing nails. Cut notches in underside of rafters to fit top band as necessary.

Step 14: Measure the space between the insides of the end rafters and divide by 3. Use this number to mark the center of the middle two rafters. Fasten them to the ridge board and the top band using 16-penny galvanized finishing nails.

Step 15: Rip true 2- x 2- x 70½-inch battens from 2 x 4s.

Step 16: Fasten a 2- x 2- x 70½-inch batten at the tops and bottoms of the rafters, centered on the rafters.

Step 17: Fasten the rest of the battens between the top and bottom battens equally spaced (about 4 inches apart).

Step 18: Add side posts and fencing to fit plan.

Step 19: Add posts as in Step 1, making the top of each fence post approximately the same height as the bottom of the top band.

Fence

Step 1: Determine the size of the fence, and draw a measured plan to scale on graph paper.

Step 2: Using 4 x 6s for the line posts and 6 x 6s for the corner posts, space postholes 7 feet 2½ inches on cen-ter. Carefully measure and mark the center of each posthole with a stake in the ground, using a string to check for alignment of the post marks to ensure a straight fence.

Step 3: Dig holes 12 inches in diameter and 36 inches deep for line and corner posts.

Step 4: Place several inches of small gravel (8-9-10) in the bottom of each hole, and tamp.

Step 5: Set posts in holes with 6-inch side facing outward, and plumb using a post level or a 2-foot level. Use a diagonal brace attached to the post and a stake in the ground to hold the post plumb in each direction.

Step 6: Use a string fastened between the end or corner posts to check for post alignment. Make sure all post faces are in one line and flat to the string. Adjust as needed, maintaining plumb.

Step 7: Mix and pour concrete around each post, tamping lightly to remove air bubbles. Crown the top of the concrete around each post to direct moisture away from posts. Let concrete set before continuing.

Step 8: Determine desired post height. Measure up from the ground at the end post nearest the gate, and make a mark. With a string level, transfer this mark to the remaining posts.

Step 9: Cut off the excess from each post. Then mark a 60-degree-bevel angle on each post and trim (see Fence Elevation at right).

Step 10: Begin fence panels (rails on back of posts and pickets to the front). Cut and fasten the bottom 7-foot 2½-inch rail on center between the first two posts with the bottom edge 2 inches above the ground. Check for level.

Step 11: Measure up 8 inches from the top of the bottom

rail, and mark each post. Fasten the next rail with its bottom edge on this mark. Check for level. Repeat with the next six rails. The top of the top rail should be about 7 feet above the ground.

Step 12: Size the pickets by making a mark down 4 inches from the top of each post and measuring from this mark to the bottom edge of the bottom rail. This is the picket length (about 7 feet 10 inches).

Step 13: Using the marks from Step 12, fasten a level string line to use as a guide for the top of each picket.

Step 14: Cut each picket top at a 60-degree bevel.

Step 15: Fasten the first picket centered between the posts. Align the top to the string and the bottom flush with the bottom of the bottom rail (trim as needed).

Step 16: Fasten remaining pickets, spaced equally. Repeat process for the rest of the fence.

This sturdy fence is tall enough to provide a measure of privacy for your yard, and the design makes it easy to customize for your landscape.

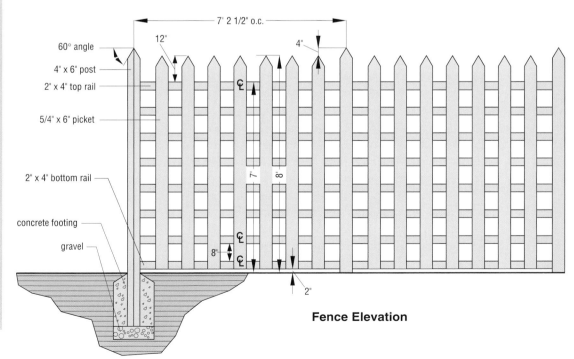

60° angle
4" x 6" post
2" x 4" top rail
5/4" x 6" picket
2" x 4" bottom rail
concrete footing
gravel

7' 2 1/2" o.c.
12"
4"
7'
8'
8"
2"

Fence Elevation

potting bench

as featured on page 64

This useful potting bench can double as a handy outdoor buffet to serve family and friends. Designed to help the gardener stay organized and the yard to stay tidy, the bench has an ample work surface, along with places to store pots, supplies, and other gardening essentials.

Instructions

Step 1: Cut all materials according to the cut list (page 123), except for the top edge band.

Step 2: Assemble frame (see illustrations at far right).

a. Mark front and back legs at 13 inches; also mark back legs at 35¼ inches.

b. Align top edge of corner anchors to the marks, and attach using 1¼-inch screws.

c. Attach two 16-inch side shelf supports to a front and back leg, top and bottom, creating one end of the bench.

d. Attach the four 48-inch top and bottom front and back supports to the completed end. (**Tip:** Use clamps to hold the supports in the anchors while you do this, making sure the ends are firmly in the anchors.)

e. Attach the remaining two front and back legs to the four 48-inch front and back shelf supports.

f. Attach the other two top and bottom 16-inch side supports to complete the frame.

g. Mark the center of all 48-inch front and back supports, and predrill holes using a ⅛-inch bit. Position the two center supports, and secure to the frame using 8-penny hot galvanized finishing nails. (See illustration on page 122.)

Step 3: Add bottom shelf.

a. Notch first board for the front and back leg. (**Tip:** Stand a scrap 2 x 2 on end at the front and back outside corners to mark a 1½- x 1½-inch notch at each of the two corners. Cut notches and dry-fit, trimming as needed.)

b. Using a ⅛-inch bit, predrill four holes in first board, each approximately ¾ inch in from each edge. This should place the screws in the center of the shelf support. Attach using four 2-inch screws per board.

c. Attach the next seven boards, predrilling each corner ¾ inch in from the outer edges, and then securing the board with 2-inch screws to the shelf supports. Keep

Lowe's Shopping List

Lumber
- 6 (8-foot) 2 x 2s
- 2 (8-foot) 1 x 2s
- 3 (8-foot) 1 x 6s
- 4 (10-foot) 1 x 6s
- 1 (8-foot) 1 x 4
- 1 (4- x 8-foot) lattice panel
- 7 (3½-inch x ½-inch) wooden shaker pegs

Hardware
- 8 corner anchors
- 1 box 1¼-inch screws
- 1 box #8 x 2 exterior wood screws
- 24 (¾-inch) exterior or brass wood screws
- 1 box 4-penny galvanized finishing nails
- 1 box 8-penny hot-dipped galvanized finishing nails

Tools
- circular saw, miter or table saw
- jigsaw
- framing square
- wood clamps
- drill with countersink pilot bit and screwdriver bit
- ½-inch spade bit
- nail gun or hammer

Miscellaneous
- 1 gallon exterior stain
- wood glue
- adhesive caulking

boards snug to one another and flush with the front and back edges of the supports.

d. Repeat steps 3a and 3b for notching and attaching the last bottom shelf board.

Step 4: Attach the top shelf boards. (**Note:** Top shelf boards will be centered on the frame.)

a. Cut a notch in the back shelf board 2¼- x 1½-inch where it will meet the back legs when centered. This will leave ¾ inch of back overhang to house the backsplash. Predrill, then secure the board to the frame with 2-inch screws, which should enter into the center of the supports.

b. Attach the next two boards in the same fashion (without notching), aligning with the back board.

c. Attach the final shelf board; note that it will overhang the front of the frame by approximately 3 inches. Predrill, then secure to side supports and front support with 2-inch screws every 6 inches.

d. Mark the center support, and predrill the shelf boards for two more screws in each board to secure them to the center support. Use only one screw at the forward end of the back shelf board.

Step 5: Construct the peg rail.

a. Mark a vertical line down the center of a 1- x 6- x 54½-inch board. On each side of this center line, mark a line at 6 inches, 12 inches, and 18 inches. Next, mark the center of each end of the board (approximately 2¾ inches), and draw a horizontal line across the length of the board using a straightedge.

b. Using a ½-inch spade bit, drill a peg hole at each point where a vertical line crosses the horizontal line. (**Tip:** Place a scrap piece of wood under board to prevent splintering.)

c. Apply a small amount of wood glue to the end of each peg, and tap them into the holes. Wipe off excess glue.

Step 6: Center and attach the peg rail, flush with top of back legs, and attach the 1 x 4 backsplash, flush with top shelf board, to the back legs using 2-inch screws. (**Tip:** Use clamps to hold boards while attaching.)

Step 7: Construct and attach the pigeonhole assembly. (See illustrations on page 122.)

a. Attach dividers to one of the three 1- x 6- x 54½-inch pigeonhole storage boards, creating the back of the unit. Predrill with a ⅛-inch bit, and use 2-inch screws and glue to attach the first two dividers on the ends, the third in the center of the board, and the last two 18 inches from the center divider.

b. Attach a second pigeonhole storage board as the top. This board will rest at an angle on top of the dividers. Caulk the back-edge gap.

Pigeonholes, shaker pegs, and lattice all add decorative touches to this potting bench. Corner anchors facilitate assembly and add rigidity to the structure.

Step 2:
Frame Construction

Step 3:
Bottom Shelf

Step 4:
Top Shelf

Step 6:
Peg Rail

WORKBOOK

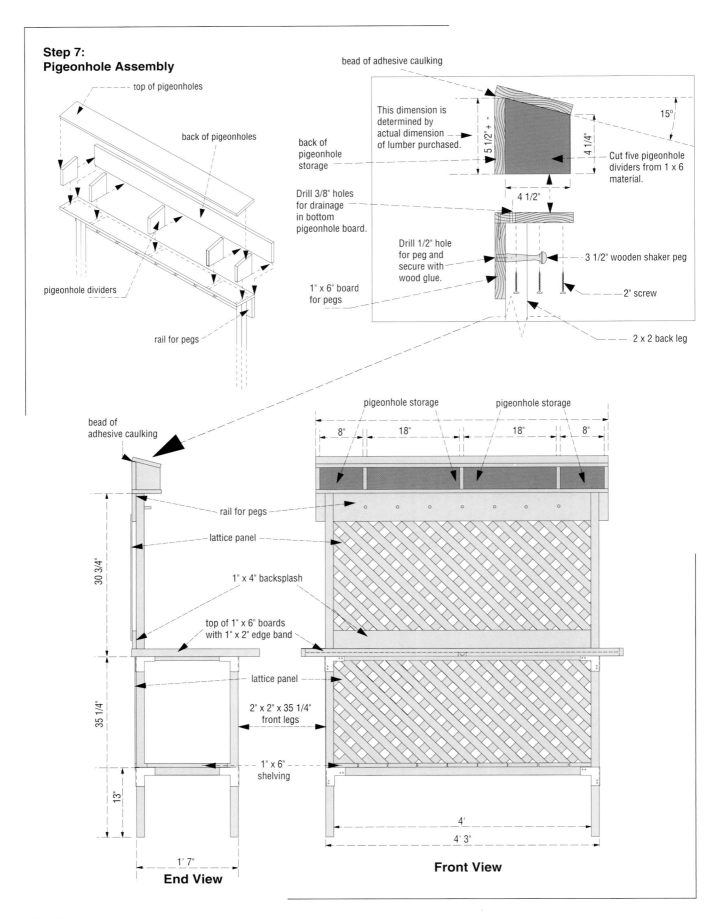

Step 7:
Pigeonhole Assembly

top of pigeonholes

back of pigeonholes

pigeonhole dividers

rail for pegs

bead of adhesive caulking

This dimension is determined by actual dimension of lumber purchased.

back of pigeonhole storage

5 1/2" +

4 1/2"

4 1/4"

15°

Cut five pigeonhole dividers from 1 x 6 material.

Drill 3/8" holes for drainage in bottom pigeonhole board.

Drill 1/2" hole for peg and secure with wood glue.

3 1/2" wooden shaker peg

1" x 6" board for pegs

2" screw

2 x 2 back leg

bead of adhesive caulking

pigeonhole storage

pigeonhole storage

8"   18"   18"   8"

rail for pegs

lattice panel

1" x 4" backsplash

top of 1" x 6" boards with 1" x 2" edge band

lattice panel

2" x 2" x 35 1/4" front legs

1" x 6" shelving

30 3/4"

35 1/4"

13"

1' 7"

End View

4'

4' 3"

Front View

c. Attach the third pigeonhole board to the top of the frame and peg rail by predrilling and using 2-inch screws and glue. Drill ⅜-inch holes in this board, as needed, for drainage. Attach the entire pigeonhole assembly from steps 7a and 7b to the pigeonhole board in step 7c by predrilling through the bottom board into the divider boards with a ⅛-inch bit, then securing with 2-inch screws and glue in each divider.

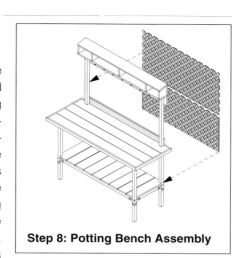

Step 8: Potting Bench Assembly

Step 8: Attach the lattice panels to the back of the bench.

a. Using the remaining 1¼-inch screws, fasten the bottom panel into the back legs.

b. With ¾-inch exterior screws, fasten the top panel into the back of the peg rail and the backsplash.

Step 9: Attach the top shelf edge bands.

a. Cut to fit the four top shelf edge band pieces, mitering corners. The two sides are approximately 24¾ inches from long point to long point; the front and back are approximately 59½ inches from long point to long point.

b. Attach using 4-penny finishing nails. (**Note:** Paint or stain bench, if desired. See "Helpful Hints" on page 121.)

CUT LIST

Part	Material	Length	Quantity	Notes
front legs	2 x 2	35¼-inch	2	
back legs	2 x 2	66 inches	2	
top and bottom, side and center shelf supports	2 x 2	16 inches	6	
top and bottom, front and back shelf supports	2 x 2	48 inches	4	
bottom shelf boards	1 x 6	19 inches	9	cut from 2" x 6" x 8'
top-edge band (cut to fit ends)	1 x 2	24¾-inch approximately	2	cut to fit ends after mitering
top-edge band (cut to fit front and back ends)	1 x 2	59½ inches approximately	2	cut to fit front and back ends after mitering
top shelf boards	1 x 6	58¼-inch	4	cut from 1" x 6" x 10'
board for pegs	1 x 6	54½-inch	1	cut from 1" x 6" x 10'
pigeonhole storage boards	1 x 6	54½-inch	3	cut from 1" x 6" x 10'
pigeonhole dividers	1 x 6	5½-inch (back); 4¼-inch (front)	5	top edge slants downward from back to front
backsplash	1 x 4	51 inches	1	
lattice top panel	lattice	51 x 24 inches	1	
lattice bottom panel	lattice	51 x 24 inches	1	

mobile lemonade stand

as featured on page 94

The neighbors are sure to line up in front of this adorable stand, and your kids will be selling lemonade in the shade.

Instructions

Step 1: Assemble the two-door cabinet according to the manufacturer's instructions.

Step 2: Gently pry away cabinet backing. Cut ½-inch-thick paint-grade plywood to 30 inches square, and attach to cabinet back with wood glue. Secure with countersunk brad nails. This adds support and stability to the cabinet.

Lowe's Shopping List

Materials
- unfinished-oak two-door wall cabinet (30 x 30 x 12 inches)
- 4-foot-square (½-inch-thick) paint-grade plywood
- wood glue
- 1 small package ¾-inch brad nails
- 1 x 6 board
- 1 (⁵⁄₄-inch-thick x 36-inch-round) tabletop
- 16 (1¾-inch) galvanized carriage bolts
- 4 (2-inch minimum) swivel industrial casters (2 locking)
- 16 lock washers, galvanized
- 16 hex nuts, galvanized
- 1 quart exterior primer
- 4 quarts of eggshell paint in four colors
- 2 (4-hook) flat bars
- spray paint
- Laura Ashley stencil
- acrylic paint for umbrella
- 1½-inch wood screws
- 2 (2-inch) wood ball knobs
- polyurethane
- 8-foot, 2-inch wood market umbrella
- closet-rod cup anchor
- 2 (20- to 40-pound) bags of sand

Tools
- circular saw
- hammer or nail set
- straight edge
- drill and bits
- measuring tape
- adjustable wrench
- screwdriver
- drop cloth
- level

A two-door cabinet is transformed into a serving station complete with wheels, storage, and shade.

Step 3: To find the center of cabinet top, use a straightedge to mark an "X" from corner to corner. Drill a 1½-inch-diameter hole at the center point. Do the same for the middle shelf. (**Note:** Umbrella poles may vary in diameter, so measure yours, and drill accordingly.) Place the tabletop on top of the cabinet. Use a measuring tape to center the tabletop, then mark the cabinet corners on it. Connect the corners with an "X" to find the approximate center of the tabletop, and drill a hole for the umbrella at the center point.

Step 4: Turn cabinet upside down, and glue four 6-inch-square blocks (cut from a 1 x 6) to the bottom corners to fill the lip and form a base for the casters.

Step 5: Drill pilot holes through corner blocks and cabinet base for casters. Using 1¾-inch galvanized carriage bolts, affix casters to cabinet base on the outside. Secure with lock washers and hex nuts on the inside.

Step 6: Patch any holes in cabinet surfaces with wood filler, if desired. Prime all pieces of the cabinet except its top, and prime the top of the tabletop.

Step 7: Paint the cabinet front with your favorite colors. We used a citrus theme of orange, lime green,

Painted hooks installed on the cabinet's sides provide space for basket, hand towels, and other necessities. Use a stencil to embellish the tabletop, or draw a freehand design of your own.

and lemon yellow, accented with touches of black.

Step 8: Paint the tabletop using stencil and home-made designs as desired.

Step 9: Using 1½-inch wood screws and predrilling, attach the tabletop from the inside of the cabinet. (**Tip:** Before attaching, place umbrella through center hole down to bottom to check alignment.)

Step 10: Spray-paint the 4-hook flat bars and wooden knobs, and attach to cabinet when dry. (**Note:** Drill a hole ¼ inch to the outside of the original hole to allow for new knob size.)

Step 11: Apply a coat of clear polyurethane to the entire piece to protect the finish.

Step 12: Using a drop cloth to protect the work area, lay the umbrella canvas on a flat surface.

Step 13: Paint stripes and a scallop design using acrylic paints. Use stencils to add a decorative touch to the top and coordinate it with the tabletop.

Step 14: Saw approximately 6 inches off the bottom of the umbrella pole to balance the umbrella's weight with that of the cabinet.

Step 15: Insert umbrella through top and middle shelf. Plumb the vertical line of the umbrella with a small level to be sure it is straight, and then mark the cabinet bottom for anchor placement. Attach the closet-rod cup anchor to hold the umbrella in place. These anchors vary in size, so check your umbrella carefully for fit. Place two 20- to 40-pound bags of sand in the bottom of the cabinet for stability.

STANDARD SIZES

LUMBER SIZES

Nominal	Actual
1 x 2	¾ x 1½
1 x 4	¾ x 3½
1 x 6	¾ x 5½
1 x 8	¾ x 7¼
1 x 10	¾ x 9¼
1 x 12	¾ x 11¼
2 x 2	1½ x 1½
2 x 4	1½ x 3½
2 x 6	1½ x 5½
2 x 8	1½ x 7¼
2 x 10	1½ x 9¼
2 x 12	1½ x 11¼
4 x 4	3½ x 3½
4 x 6	3½ x 5½
6 x 6	5½ x 5½
8 x 8	7½ x 7½

NAIL SIZES

length in inches	penny size
1	2d
1¼	3d
1½	4d
1¾	5d
2	6d
2¼	7d
2½	8d
2¾	9d
3	10d
3¼	12d
3½	16d
4	20d

SCREW SIZES

gauge	shank diameter	length
4	$7/64$	⅜"-1"
6	$9/64$	½"-2"
8	$5/32$	½"-3"
10	$3/16$	¾"-3½"
12	$7/32$	¾"-3½"

INDEX

AT LOWE'S...
we're here for you!

Because of our commitment to customer service, Lowe's has expanded its offerings to help homeowners complete their renovations and projects. Here are the top 10 ways in which Lowe's can help you with your home improvement endeavors.

1 Professionals install. Upgrades such as flooring, plumbing fixtures, and cabinetry require knowledge and time. Lowe's can provide guaranteed professional installation.

2 Just ask us, and we'll order it. Take advantage of our Special Order Services. With access to more than 250,000 products, you're bound to find whatever item you're seeking.

3 We offer payment options. Take a look at Lowe's Consumer Credit Card as an option to finance your next project. Apply by visiting Lowes.com and clicking "Credit," or simply drop by the store nearest you for an application.

4 We assist. We deliver, and we can provide guaranteed professional installation.

5 We match your colors. Bring a sample to Lowe's, and our computers will create a matching paint shade in minutes.

6 We guarantee our prices. Our everyday low-price guarantee eliminates comparison shopping. If we find an identical item priced lower elsewhere, we will match the price. Should we happen to miss one, we will take off an additional 10%.

7 Our return policy is hassle free. If you are not completely happy with your purchase, simply return it, along with your original sales receipt, to any local Lowe's store within 90 days.* We'll either repair it, replace it, refund your money, or credit your account.

*30 days for outdoor power equipment (chain saws, blowers, tillers, trimmers, mowers, and pressure washers)

8 We offer friendly service. If you have any questions about a project, ask our knowledgeable staff. They'll be happy to find a solution within our store. Browse through additional projects at Lowes.com.

9 Our experts teach you how. Check out our free How-To Clinics on every subject from installing ceramic tile to organizing storage space. For more information and to sign up, visit your local Lowe's store, or go to Lowes.com/Clinics.

How-To CLINICS

10 We guarantee our plants. If a plant doesn't survive for a year after purchase, return it to your local store with the receipt, and we'll replace it.

1 YEAR GUARANTEE ON EVERY PLANT